THE MANAGER'S GUIDE TO SALES INCENTIVES

THE MANAGER'S GUIDE TO SALES INCENTIVES

Gerald E. Bullus

Gower

Published by
Gower Publishing Company Limited
Aldershot, Hants, England

British Library Cataloguing in Publication Data

Bullus, Gerald E.
  The manager's guide to sales incentives
  1. Sales personnel—Salaries, commissions, etc.
  2. Incentives in industry
  I. Title
  685.3'225   HF5439.7

ISBN 0–566–02353–9

Contents

Types of motivation. Whom do you hope to motivate? Why salesmen need motivating. What motivates a salesman? How to motivate salesmen. What demotivates salesmen? The importance of communication. Management motivation checklist. Common causes of demotivation. Designing an effective sales pay plan. Elements of a comprehensive pay package. Types of sales pay plan. Other types of motivator. Sales motivation audit.

How to design, plan and promote an effective sales incentive campaign. Typical sales incentives. When to use incentives. Incentive travel the prime motivator? 'Motivate Sales Teams with Travel'. 'Travel – tomorrow's Prime Motivator'.

Objectives.
1 Increase sales. 2 Increase profits. 3 Improve sales efficiency. 4 Encourage sales teamwork. 5 Obtain customer recommendations.

6 Stimulate new sales ideas. 7 Test product knowledge. 8 Increase new business prospecting. 9 New product launch. 10 Improve customer relations. 11 Promote special products or services. 12 Boost salesmen's morale.

Motor trade dealer incentive campaign. Marketing incentives in the electronics industry. Cosmetics company – a typical incentive campaign.

A typical marketing plan. How to use incentives in achieving marketing objectives. Sales force objectives. Promotional support. The sales promotion activity plan. Monitoring and measuring. Refining and improving sales incentive schemes.

When to press the 'Go' button. Leadership and motivation. Public relations and incentives. Reviewing incentives that failed. Answers to questionnaire.

The changing status of the salesman. Motivation – a management art. Buying incentive experience. The last word.

Preface

To help managers to understand what motivates salesmen. To help them to use this knowledge in a practical
way to raise the work rate of salesmen.

These are the main objectives of this book.

Using sales incentives to encourage extra effort.
Achieving better standards of sales performance. Making
extra profit from extra sales. Paying for the incentives out
of this extra profit. These are good enough reasons to justify the use of sales incentives.

The sales manager who introduces sales incentives in
his company for the first time will quickly learn that motivation is a complex subject. First, he needs the support of
an efficient sales office. Too often, sales incentives don't
work because of poor communications or a lack of accurate
information. Regular monitoring of sales performance.
Frequent progress reports. Updating information. Con-
tinuous promotion. They are all key elements in the operation of a professional sales incentive campaign. Even the
most imaginative ideas can only succeed if they are to be
implemented efficiently.

'Incentive' and 'motivate' have very similar meanings.
These words, in the field of selling, are often inter-
changed. 'Incentivise' has recently crept into sales jargon.
(Definition – prod, spur, goad, big stick.) 'Motivate' has
long been in use (move, actuate, manipulate, driving
force). If one thinks of the force which wields the stick, the
former is motivating and the latter is incentivising and
that's roughly the difference between the two. Not that we
are proposing management by violence. Although many a
manager will have been tempted by the thought, when
faced with the problems of an unwilling salesman and an
unbending sales objective!

To increase profits may be the main objective of a sales incentive campaign, designed to motivate salesmen. This won't necessarily be the only benefit. For example, a well run sales incentive will often force an organisation to become more efficient. Accurate statistics, analysis of results, expediting customer orders, control and distribution of information, are all facets of the corporate system likely to require polishing during a sales incentive campaign. Many other lasting benefits can result from the use of incentives as a motivational tool. Salesmen will more willingly accept discipline when offered a reward for their pains. Sales time is more likely to be fully utilised, with report writing and sales planning kept outside usual customer call hours. Recruitment can be easier, particularly if the company takes advantage of publicising regular details of sales successes, thus improving its image at the expense of competition. Training courses will be approached with more enthusiasm by salesmen keen to learn more about company products in order to enhance their chances of sales success. One surprising benefit resulted when a manufacturing company introduced an incentive scheme for its three distributors' salesmen. Only two distributors took up the offer and increased their sales as a result. The third distributor, provoked by the success of his rivals, ordered more stock than he had ever bought before. The manufacturer thus increased his sales to all three distributors and was well satisfied with the profitable result.

Today, incentives play a most important role within the company marketing plan. The cost of sales failure in a tough environment is becoming an experience few companies can afford. An incentive which results in increased sales, without affecting fixed costs, is every sales manager's dream. Attention to a number of well established ground rules, combined with an imaginative approach, can help to make the dream a reality.

I've found it easier to refer to 'salespersons' as 'salesmen' in this book. Also, it's less clumsy to use 'he' and 'his' than 'he/she', 'his/her' etc. I have trouble enough with my grammar without these male and female complications!

There is no other reason for leaving women out of the book. I've met many successful saleswomen, and have a very special regard for any woman who takes up this arduous profession. Many sales managers don't have the courage to employ women in their sales teams. They prefer to avoid the responsibility. If a saleswoman fails, the manager may be blamed for his irresponsible policy of daring to introduce a woman into a 'man's world'. Times are changing too slowly, but I look forward to the day when many more sales managers wear skirts.

Gerry Bullus

Acknowledgements

Grateful thanks are due to World's Work Ltd, The Windmill Press, Kingswood, Tadworth, Surrey, UK publishers of Dale Carnegie's *How to Win Friends and Influence People* for permission to quote from this book, and to I.S.E. Publications Ltd, 13 Vaughan Road, Harpenden, Herts., for permission to reproduce the extracts from *Sales and Marketing Management*, in Part I.

Part I
Sales Incentives in Context

Motivating the Sales Force

The sales manager's job is to achieve company sales objectives. He has the best chance of doing this if the sales force perform to their expected levels of achievement, or sales productivity. In the job of selling, the responsibility for productivity depends very much on the efforts of the individual. If the salesman can be influenced to make an extra effort, the results can be rewarding, sometimes spectacular.

The skilful manager uses motivational techniques to obtain that extra effort from salesmen. Motivation can provide the driving force to turn an average salesperson into a star performer. Then, having enjoyed the pleasures of success, the new 'star' will probably want the experience to continue.

The 'motivation key' can be craftsman-made in the hands of a skilled manager. It can be used time and again to unlock the doors to success for individuals. But the manager who uses it has to be sure it works. He needs to know and understand the people he wishes to motivate.

Definition: 'Motivation is the art of influencing a sales-man *willingly* to make extra efforts to increase personal sales efficiency and productivity.' The reasons which make people respond to motivational techniques are as complex as human behaviour. The theory and psychology of motivation can be studied elsewhere. Here, the aim is to focus on the practical ways in which a manager can help sales people perform to the heights of their ability. No one can be expected to work beyond their own capabilities. Unfortunately, salesmen usually work well below their true levels of ability. Because of the lonely nature of the job, they often have to work unsupervised and un-supported. Maintaining a high work rate in these circumstances calls for grit, determination and self-discipline. Discipline imposed by management in the form of reports, controls or quotas, can certainly play an important part. Include motivation as an additional management tool and you introduce a new dimension to the selling effort. Results produced by an efficient, con-trolled, well motivated sales team will prove superior to a team lacking this exciting 'plus factor'. In an increas-ingly competitive world, business failure is becoming commonplace. To stay ahead, a business needs to keep a competitive edge. This edge can be provided by a dynamic sales team, motivated by a manager who aims to use their energies to the full.

Types of motivation

There are two types of motivation, financial and non-financial. Too many managers still stick to the outdated opinion that money is all that is needed to motivate sales-men. Many salesmen will also claim that they're moti-vated best by money. This simply isn't true. Financial in-centives on their own are too limited as a motivational tool. The many alternatives are discussed in later chap-ters, as are various remuneration schemes, which are re-commended for use in conjunction with a sound pay plan.

Whom do you hope to motivate?

The responsible manager will want to be sure that motivation will work for his sales force. He'll need to employ
people who are likely to respond favourably to his motivational ideas, to select and train salesmen who have the
basic ability to do a good job. This is a top priority management function. Sales ability is more important than
knowledge of the product to be sold. The search for the best
people with the right attitude of mind is of paramount importance. Set a high standard. Take as much time and
care as necessary to ensure that, as far as possible, the
right person is selected for the job. Don't accept the best
candidate from a poor application list unless they meet
the standard. The sales manager is only as good as the
salesmen he employs (and hopes to motivate)! The current
failure rate of salesmen in industry is too high and too
costly. Lost sales, damaged morale, bad company image,
and increased recruitment and training requirements,
can result in horrific additions to sales expenses. Recruitment should follow a strict pattern of efficient routine.
Then, armed with all the facts, the manager should use
his experience and judgement to make the final choice.
There should be no shortcuts. For example, many of the
salesmen employed today don't have their credentials or
references properly checked by their prospective employer. The best possible way to obtain accurate references is
to pick up the telephone and call previous employers.
Executives are far more likely to discuss confidential matters informally in this way, than commit themselves in
writing. A carefully selected employee will respect the
manager making the selection. It's logical to expect that
people can be motivated more easily when they respect
the manager responsible for this activity.

Why salesmen need motivating

What happens when the resilient, cheerful character we
employed becomes depressed and apathetic? After all, he's

only human. Perhaps, through no fault of his own, he fails to win orders. He's used to the ups and downs, the exhilaration and the disappointment, the cut and thrust of competition. Then he's hit by a whole series of downs. He loses orders because of poor delivery, or cut price competition from cheap imports, or quality control problems. No clever commission scheme will raise his enthusiasm. Criticism will only further dampen his spirit. He needs management help. A creative motivation scheme could rejuvenate his morale. For example, a wise manager, knowing that business will eventually recover, could offer rewards for increasing sales call rates. The salesman is thus encouraged to 'work through' the bad patch. The pressure to obtain immediate sales is lifted and replaced by a new challenge – increasing the call rate.

The job of a salesman in the field calls for above average ability and determination. The salesman who calls on prospective customers is likely to fail more often than he succeeds. Usually, because of his personality and ego drive, failure will act as a trigger. He makes greater efforts to achieve success on his next call, to satisfy his ego. He pictures himself as successful, he is driven by the need to identify with the picture. Failure over a long period could destroy the successful self picture from which his ego drive draws its energy. The shrewd manager will recognise the problem and take action to avoid the situation. Long periods away from home can also cause a salesman to get depressed and lose that vital spark. Motivation can compensate for some of these less acceptable aspects of the selling job.

Confusion of loyalty is another cause of emotional stress which could lead to a fall off in sales performance. Suppose the salesman forms a close friendship with a customer. He may find himself taking sides with the customer against the company. He returns to base, and realises that a conflict of interests has occurred. He now wishes to identify with the company. Inexperienced salesmen sometimes have to face this problem, which could impair their efficiency and attitude to work. Additional motivation may be useful to help remind them of their first loyaly to their employer.

Travelling around the same territory with the same product year in, year out, can cause a salesman to get into a rut. In these circumstances he needs to be constantly re-enthused. Motivational techniques can generate new interest in a dull routine. The salesman working a territory on his own would like to feel that he was a member of an enthusiastic and successful team. He'd like to meet his colleagues regularly in a spirit of fellowship. The problem for management is to create this climate and persuade remote members of a sales force that they are involved in a collective endeavour. In such circumstances, motivation can be an aid to creating team spirit. The individuals will not wish to let down their 'team' by a poor performance, which may be made public. Therefore, they strive extra hard to meet team performance standards.

Sometimes a salesman may need to be motivated to remind him that selling is his most important function. He may prefer to see himself primarily as an engineer, advisor, technician or consultant. The job of selling may have become confused with another less important function, or he may attempt to cover his lack of sales success by exaggerating the importance of some secondary activity. The manager on such occasions has to influence the salesman back in the right direction. It's important that his ego is satisfied mostly by success in selling. This is the main purpose of his job. That's why he may need motivating.

What motivates a salesman?

A salesman has individual needs which can be satisfied by the job of selling. These needs vary and may manifest themselves in different ways. The manager who understands the individual needs of his salesmen is in the best position to motivate. If he can influence them to make extra efforts to achieve success and self esteem in their jobs he is most likely to obtain performances and work rates from them which are nearer to their true capability.

Some salesmen are better than others because they respond better to motivation, and therefore make more effort to succeed.

The conscious and subconscious needs of salesmen will determine the ways in which they react. Achieving fulfilment of these needs influences their reactions and behaviour. So what are the needs? We shall assume that the salesmen's basic needs are already satisfied, i.e. the person is reasonably settled in society, enjoys at least an average standard of living and feels fairly secure in the job. Otherwise, it's unlikely that he can be made to respond to motivation which is based on other less basic needs. These other needs are:

1 The need to belong and be accepted as equal with colleagues at work (and sometimes in their home environment also).
2 The need to achieve goals which will win the approval, recognition, and respect of others (self esteem).
3 The need to do an honest day's work (most people need to work to feel satisfied. Salesmen, in particular, can quickly become demotivated if they don't keep busy).
4 The need to achieve self-fulfilment.

Each individual will have different need priorities. They will respond with varying degrees of effort to motivational devices. For example, one person (perhaps an older salesman) will have already achieved recognition and respect. He can only be motivated by some kind of incentive which will enable him to achieve self-fulfilment. A junior salesman, on the other hand, is more likely to yearn for acceptance by his colleagues at work. He may also be striving for equal status with his friends in his social environment. The implication for management is plain. Opportunities must be provided for salesmen to realise their secondary needs. Then they can motivate sales performance levels and obtain the extra effort required to achieve above average success. Carefully planned incentive schemes designed to take into account the needs of each individual, can go a long way to achiev-ing this objective. But the manager must know and understand his staff well before he can plan his strategy. Skill in human relations is vital in this situation. The manager who is good at dealing with people is good at motivating people.

The rewards for motivating salesmen can be miracul-ous. The story of the hillbilly who came to the big city from the farm in the country has been told many times, but is still worth repeating. He applied for a job as a trainee salesman, selling trucks with a big town dealer. In spite of the competition from dozens of much better qualified applicants he got the job. There was a special quality of enthusiasm about him which the sales manager couldn't resist. He'd 'always had a hankerin' to sell trucks'. After the usual period of training (where he demonstrated a keenness never previously equalled by any recruit), he was let loose on his territory. His determination, en-thusiasm, and work rate soon produced results which placed him high in the sales league. His 'hankerin'' was satisfied and he contentedly settled down in his new care-er, performing consistently well enough to hold his own with more senior salesmen in the dealership. Then the manufacturer introduced an incentive, offering a reward of a ten-day all expenses paid trip to London for the win-ning salesman. Our hero 'had a hankerin'' to go. He pro-ceeded to sell more trucks than all the other salesmen put together. He went to London. Later he visited many exotic places in the world and great were the rewards he enjoyed from the various sales incentive competitions which he continually strove to win. He didn't understand the theories of motivation. All he was aware of was that he 'had a hankerin'' feeling which provided him with the driving force to make efforts far beyond expected levels.

The manager who searches for opportunities to moti-vate his salesmen won't always be successful. However, he has a much better chance of success if he takes the time and trouble to find out what motivates his salesmen.

How to motivate salesmen

We have discussed briefly the psychological needs of salesmen. Knowledge of these needs will help a manager in his ideas to motivate salesmen. The use of incentives as motivators is recommended. The subject is dealt with at length later in this book. However, the manager who wishes to motivate his salesmen would do well also to study human behaviour and the art of dealing with people. He'll think of many instances where motivating salesmen can be accomplished without any cost to the company in terms of financial or material rewards for increased effort. There are fundamental techniques in the art of dealing with people which managers regularly use on customers, then for some strange reason, they disregard them when dealing with their own salesmen.

The finest book ever written on the art of dealing with people is Dale Carnegie's *How to win friends and influence people*. No salesmen or manager should consider his education complete without reading and rereading this book. It's as practical, topical and true today as it was when first published. There are many useful tips by Carnegie, summarised below, which would help managers to understand what motivates a salesman. Practical managers will recognise the truth in Carnegie's words. They serve as a useful reminder to all managers. They contain so many common sense ideas which will help managers to use efficiently the techniques of motivation.

'There is only one way under high Heaven to get anybody to do anything. Did you ever stop to think of that? Yes, just one way. And that is by making the other person want to do it. Remember, there is no other way.'

The manager who can motivate his salesmen to want to achieve something strongly enough has a most powerful tool at his command.

'But there is one longing almost as deep, almost as imperious, as the desire for food or sleep, which is seldom gratified. It is what Freud calls "The desire to be great". It is what Dewey calls "The desire to be important". Lincoln *once began a letter by saying: "Everybody likes a compliment", William James said: "The deepest principle in human nature is the craving to be appreciated."*

This message refers to the 'self esteem' need which motivates human behaviour.

The chapter continues to focus attention on this very important subject. Carnegie refers to the special ability of Charles Schwab, a million dollar a year executive, successful because of his fantastic skills in dealing with people. He quotes Schwab as saying:

' *"I consider my ability to arouse enthusiasm among the men", said Schwab, "the greatest asset I possess, and the way to develop the best that is in a man is by appreciation and encouragement. There is nothing else that so kills the ambitions of a man as criticisms from his superiors. I never criticise anyone. I believe in giving a man incentives to work. So I am anxious to praise, but loath to find fault. If I like anything, I am hearty in my appreciation and lavish in my praise". That is what Schwab does. But what does the average man do? The exact opposite. If he doesn't like a thing he raises the Old Harry; if he does like it, he says nothing.'*

Carnegie emphasises the point with further comment:

'We nourish the bodies of our children and friends and employees; but how seldom do we nourish their self esteem. We provide them with roast beef and potatoes to build energy; but we neglect to give them kind words of appreciation that would sing in their memories for years, like the music of the morning stars.'

The next point is an important point for salesmen to remember, but equally important for the managers who are interested in motivation. After a story which stresses the importance of talking about what the other person wants (because that's what he's really interested in) he continues:

'Why talk about what we want? This is childish. Absurd, of course you are interested in what you want. You are eter-

nally interested in it. But no one else is. The rest of us are just like you, we are interested in what we want. So the only way on earth to influence the other fellow is to talk about what he wants and show him how to get it.'

The message is clear for the sales manager. He must be sure to consider what his salesmen want, then design his motivation strategy to satisfy such wants as far as he possibly can.

'So if you want to influence people to your way of thinking, Rule 7 is: LET THE OTHER FELLOW FEEL THAT THE IDEA IS HIS.'

Lesson for today's sales manager: When you develop ideas aimed at motivating your salesmen, if possible, do it in a way which enables them to feel they have developed the ideas themselves.

'There is a reason why the other man thinks and acts as he does. Ferret out that hidden reason – and you have the key to his actions, perhaps to his personality.

Try honestly to put yourself in his place.'

Back to the reasons for human behaviour, so vital to successful motivation.

Carnegie refers to motivating men by challenge of competition and refers again to his friend who was such a successful employer of people.

'Let Charles Schwab say it in his own words, "The way to get things done", says Schwab, "is to stimulate competition. I do not mean in a sordid money making way, but in the desire to excel."

'The desire to excel! The challenge! Throwing down the gauntlet! An infallible way of appealing to men of spirit. So if you want to win – spirited men, men of mettle – to your way of thinking, Rule 12 is this: THROW DOWN A CHALLENGE.'

It would seem that this piece of advice from the sage indicates that sales contests are a must for the ambitious manager.

It follows that motivating salesmen certainly doesn't always mean offering expensive rewards in return for extra effort. There are several examples here of how salesmen can be motivated by a genuine, understanding, caring, sympathetic manager. There are still many things in this world money can't buy, and that includes the business world.

What demotivates salesmen?

If a salesman isn't given a fair commission deal or a fair sales target, if he's unfairly treated or not given proper recognition – then he's likely to react in a way which will produce a demotivating effect. Managers should be sure to remove demotivating factors before preparing plans to motivate their salesmen.

Negative motivation causes 'aggro' amongst the sales force. The signs to watch for are:

Aggression – against individuals or against the company.

Gall – a sour attitude from the individual affected.

Grumpiness – an irritable discontented manner, perhaps leading to an introverted sullen reaction.

Regression – a loss of enthusiasm and apparent change of character expressing itself by an attitude of resigned disinterest.

Obsession – continual references to the problem causing the person discontent or frustration.

Any unusual or out of character behaviour by an individual should be analysed for the cause. If 'aggro' is left to develop it will become more difficult to put matters right later. It may of course, be caused by some external or domestic problem which the manager is unable to control. But the lesson again is that to become a good motivator the manager will need to get to know his salesmen very well.

Nowadays, The ~~team~~ communication is an important factor of
the success of a manager, in 1992 it will be
~~even more~~
even mor
importa

The *importance* of communication

It's important that good communications exist between the ~~salesmen and their~~ manager. Failure to communicate efficiently can result in poor morale, inefficiency, and low ~~sales~~ productivity. Misunderstandings can develop and cause grievances which affect ~~a salesman's~~ performance.

a manager and his staff

the whole business

A dictatorial approach by the ~~sales~~ manager can also affect a ~~salesman's~~ attitude to the job. Communication should be a two-way process. The opportunity to iron out problems and have frank discussions with management should be provided. Good communication should mean freedom of self expression. The opportunity to present ideas and talk over problems in a friendly atmosphere. An important part of the manager's job is helping ~~his sales-men to sell~~. He wants to be sure there are no obstacles to close co-operation.

link

staff in their ~~sector~~ too

business

Personal contact with members of a large ~~sales force~~ can be difficult, but time should be set aside for this important routine. ~~It may be impractical for top sales executives to visit all salesmen in their territory. In these cases, informal interviews at national or regional sales meetings can provide an opportunity for the salesmen to talk.~~ Meeting the top manager can in itself become a motivating factor for ~~the salesman~~. He may be keen to impress, and demonstrate this by improving his performance in the future.

an employee

for

At the very least, regular telephone calls should be made to individuals. Care should be taken to ensure that constructive discussion takes place and a personnel file should be at hand for quick and accurate reference. The whole image is spoilt if for example the manager asks, 'How is your little girl getting on?', when the ~~salesman~~ *employee* happens to be the proud father of two sons. Obviously, on occasions when criticism is unavoidable, or a reprimand is necessary, the telephone becomes a very inadequate instrument indeed.

There are many hazards in written communications, yet effective use of the written word can be a powerful aid to motivation. It's perhaps surprising, that managers who take infinite care in planning and preparing an effective sales meeting, often neglect to analyse the potential motivational impact of their correspondence. Daily, letters, reports, memos, instructions, bulletins are churned out from their offices hurriedly, sometimes to the total confusion of the recipient. This famous example by the officer issuing an order to his troops offers amusing food for thought:

Colonel to the Executive Officer: At nine o'clock tomorrow there will be an eclipse of the sun, something which does not occur every day. Get the men to fall out in the company street in their fatigues so they will be able to see this rare phenomenon, and I will explain it to them. In case of rain, we will not be able to see anything, so take the men to the gym.

The Executive Officer to the Captain: By order of the Colonel tomorrow at nine o'clock there will be an eclipse of the sun; if it rains you will not be able to see it from the company's street, so then, in fatigues, the eclipse of the sun will take place in the gym, something that does not occur every day.

The Captain to the Lieutenant: By order of the Colonel in fatigues tomorrow, at nine o'clock in the morning, the eclipse of the sun will take place in the gym. The Colonel will give the order if it should rain, something which occurs every day.

The Lieutenant to the Sergeant: Tomorrow at nine o'clock the Colonel in fatigues will eclipse the sun in the gym, as it occurs every day if it is a nice day; if it rains, then in the company street.

The Sergeant to the Corporal: Tomorrow at nine the eclipse of the Colonel in fatigues will take place by cause of the sun. If it rains in the gym, something which does not take place every day, you will fall out in the company street.

Comments among the Privates: Tomorrow if it rains, it looks as if the sun will eclipse the Colonel in the gym. It is a shame that this does not occur every day.

Writing letters is an art well worth studying by the

manager hoping for effective communication with his ~~salesmen~~ staff. A good personal letter, designed to encourage a ~~salesman~~ employee in the field can work wonders for his morale and enthusiasm. It's worth making a short note beforehand, summarising the main purpose of the proposed letter and listing the points which the writer intends to raise. Two short, clear letters could prove much more effective than one long rambling epistle.

The best possible use of letters as a motivational tool can be the congratulatory letter for meritorious performance such as landing an important order, ~~exceeding a sales target~~, or doing well with a new product launch. Coming from the chairman, president, or other top executive, this letter will be cherished. It may be shown to business colleagues, family and friends. The benefit to morale and self esteem will last long after the deed has passed into history.

So, internal communication is essential for a team to be efficient.

But in 1992 managers will see changes in the external communication because the single market involves different languages.

Thus the managers of today won't be able to be the managers of tomorrow without 1 or 2 fluent foreign languages.

Management motivation checklist

- Establish clear sales objectives, mutually agreed with each salesman. ✓

- Set high personal standards and make it known that the same high standards are expected from the sales team.

- Make each salesman understand the importance of his job, and explain how he fits into the organisational scheme of things.

- Treat salesmen with consideration and respect.

- Show pride in the company and look for opportunities to regularly 'sell' the company to the salesmen.

- Let them know that the company is proud of its sales team.

- Always ensure that salesmen's efforts are recognised and regularly rewarded.

- Encourage a friendly atmosphere. Create a happy working environment.

- Monitor each salesman's performance against target and let him know the results. Then make the results public in the form of a leader board or league table. *targets*

- Offer salesmen opportunities to progress and point out ways in which they can do this.

- Involve salesmen in decision-making processes. Encourage them to make suggestions and discuss ideas to improve sales.

- Encourage self development by salesmen. Point out ways of self improvement, explaining how this can be achieved.

- Introduce excitement through regular incentives and sales contests.

- Sort out grievances – fast.

- Give salesmen as much responsibility as possible.

- Praise in public, criticise in private.

- Make them want to do what is required of them by selling them on the benefits.

- Treat salesmen like mature people and expect a mature response.

- Always explain the reasons behind company policies.

- Generate a team spirit amongst the sales team.

- When salesmen are at fault, show them how they can improve if the fault is corrected.

- Give recognition to wives (where appropriate). Aim to show a sincere interest in the supporting role of a salesman's wife.

- Show loyalty to the sales team. Be prepared to stand up and fight on their behalf.

- Make suggestions instead of issuing instructions.

The experience of the manager and the relationship between him and his sales team can make or break the best motivation plans.

For example, it's important that the manager should take time to think through a problem before making a hasty decision which could perhaps damage the morale of his salesmen. A tolerant manager thinks about the effects of communicating, sometimes at a distance, with salesmen in the field. Problems which could be sorted out in a few minutes of frank face to face discussion can be badly mishandled on the telephone. The mature manager doesn't mind admitting a few personal mistakes – his salesmen will feel better about discussing their mistakes if they know the boss makes a few of his own. Keeping promises, playing fair, exercising authority through respect, not fear, are other important attributes that a manager needs to develop before he can call himself a good motivator.

Sarcasm has no place in the good motivator's repertoire. Making a salesman look silly in front of his colleagues might seem a good joke at the time, but it can do irreparable harm to a man's enthusiasm. Reasoned argument, clear logic, and the patience to take time to explain are other elements in the human relations equation which managers need to apply before they can become professional motivators.

Common causes of demotivation

Discontent can become a serious demotivation factor, damaging morale, and affecting sales force attitude. Sales managers who have ambitions to be top motivators should look out for these common causes:

- Lack of genuine interest in salesmen by management.

What else needs to be done to motivate the workforce

● Poor and uncomfortable working conditions, e.g. worn out car, poor office facilities.

● Issuing orders in a dictatorial manner without any reason.

● Issuing ambiguous instructions that could lead to mistakes.

● Allowing unfriendly relationships between individual salesmen to affect morale of the team.

● Not enough supervision of salesmen's work and activities.

● No clearly defined standards.

● Bad examples set by managers, e.g. long lunches, fiddled expenses.

● Not giving praise when it's well earned.

● Favouritism towards individual salesmen in a team.

● Failure to keep promises.

● The use of coercion and threats.

● Bad planning.

● Absence of leadership.

● Taking credit for other people's good ideas.

● Placing blame unfairly.

● Unfair division of territories.

● Unfair commission system.

● Unfair allocation of company cars.

● Slow payment of commission.

● Lack of information.

The manager needs to keep in close touch with his salesmen and be alert for danger signals such as arguments or complaints. Sympathetic attention and prompt action to put things right can avoid major problems. Be a good listener and always try to find the real reason behind a grievance. Use firm but fair discipline. It's possible to be tough and friendly. A manager should aim to be liked by his salesmen, but not at the cost of poor discipline.

Designing an effective sales pay plan

It has been stated already that money on its own is not a good motivator. Once an individual reaches a certain level of earnings, when he's secure in the job and enjoying a good standard of living, money has a declining influence. Nevertheless the pay plan is an essential part of the total motivation package.

There are three important factors in a sales pay plan:

- It should provide a living wage.
- It should be adjustable (up or down) according to performance.
- It should offer a future possibility of progressing to higher earnings through personal performance.

Pay plans should be designed to meet different circumstances, taking into account different company needs. For example, a retail salesman in a store would expect to be paid differently from, say, a life insurance salesman.

Start with an accurate job description

Every salesman should have a formal job description which reflects his various duties. It should include the objectives the company aims to achieve and what he is expected to do to accomplish these.

Company policies which could affect a salesman in his job should be considered. For example, a new, tough line on customer credit control. Pricing policy. Distribution policy. Advertising and promotional programmes. In larger companies, job evaluation methods are used to grade each job according to the duties and responsibilities, usually allocating points to each job function. Sales jobs can be evaluated in the same way, making comparisons wherever possible with those duties or responsibilities which are similar to more general aspects of the job. For example, a salesman who has responsibility for collecting debts should have that part of the job graded on the same scale as a credit controller in another department.

Requirements of a good pay plan

The sales pay plan should be designed as an aid to motivation and not a substitute for a complete programme. It shouldn't conflict with business ethics, or pressure the salesman into selling goods regardless of suitability. For example, a salesman should not be too strongly tempted to 'upsell'. A product which is beyond the probable requirements of the customer should not be foisted upon him to enable the salesman to increase his commission.

It's rarely necessary to design a completely new pay plan from scratch. Usually, a few carefully considered revisions will meet with less resistance, and prove more effective than a complete re-hash of an existing plan. For example, it would be very difficult to switch from a salary only pay plan to a commission only system. Prior to introduction of changes, care should be taken to explain the details and sell the benefits to the salesmen.

In an extreme situation, where sales force morale has dropped to a dangerously low level, also in the case of a new company or division set up to market a specialist product, a complete new pay plan has to be designed. Management should make a comprehensive study of the market, types of potential customer, competition and the complex nature of the job. If doubts about potential sales may exist, it's better to introduce a trial pay plan. Make it clear to the sales force that the aim is to test the plan before final implementation. Probably the best solution would be to operate it for six months and review, with a final revision after twelve months.

Summary

- It should provide a living wage
- It should be fair to all concerned
- It should be easy to understand
- It should be easy to administer
- It should not create barriers to the building of team spirit
- It should be designed to prevent manipulation or abuse by dishonest salesmen
- It should be flexible enough to allow for simple adjustment
- It should fit in with the total company sales objectives
- It should be at least as good as competitor's pay plans
- It should enable earnings to be on a par with competition, paying the 'going rate' for the job

Elements of a comprehensive pay package

- Basic salary or drawing account, providing a fixed income.
- Commission, to provide a regular incentive (monthly if possible).
- Bonus or profit sharing, designed to offer longer term incentive. (Desirable to provide regular estimates. Bonus *not payable* to salesmen who leave during period of operation of the bonus.)
- Added value 'fringe' benefits. For example, paid holidays, accident and sickness benefits, pension scheme, life insurance.
- Expense allowance or reimbursement. The system should be designed to work fairly and easily for the company and the salesman.

The company may not wish to include all these elements in the salesman's pay plan. It could even be unwise to do so. One method may be to start with a straight salary/com-

mission plan for junior salesmen. The next grade up may
include bonus. Top grade or senior salesmen level would
include fringe benefits.

Flexible pay plans

Within the scope of the sales pay plan, allowance should
be made for adjustments in emphasis to suit the company's marketing requirements. For example, salesmen
may be paid commission for achieving sales volume
regardless of size of order. Trends may make it more desirable for the company to reward for large orders, say to
overcome a distribution problem. The commission scheme
should be capable of adjustment to cater for this new requirement which may not result in sales increase, but will
result in a cost saving.

Other adjustments may have to be made to encourage
salesmen to call on new business prospects, promote a new
product, or assist in a merchandising promotion. Company policy regarding such adjustments should be clearly
stated in writing. In addition, salesmen should be given
detailed explanations in advance of any adjustments,
pointing out the reasons and indicating any new opportunities for them.

Implementing new or revised pay plan

The first rule is to explain the pay plan thoroughly to sales
personnel, in advance of its implementation. Details of all
changes and the likely effect. The purpose of the changes.
What the company hopes to accomplish. What's in it for
them? i.e. a reasoned explanation of the likely benefits to
the salesmen.

Written copies of the plan and working examples of how
earnings will be calculated should be presented to each
salesman. Any salesman not clear on how it will work
should have the details explained again, either individu-
ally or at a group information session. Great care should
be taken to clear up any misunderstandings. Lack of

understanding of the company sales pay plan is a frequent cause of low morale in salesmen.

Regular progress checks and further information meetings should be organised if necessary, before the first review period. This operation to be repeated before final review and complete implementation.

Types of sales pay plan

1) Straight salary

Advantages

- Simple to administer at low cost.

- More appropriate to some selling situations e.g. in jobs requiring a high proportion of non-selling activities. Some trade selling jobs where the salesman is almost entirely an order taker. Driver-salesmen. High technology salesmen. Salesmen/buyers.

- Provides management with firm control and the power to direct salesmen to sell according to manager's priorities.

- Enables salesmen to perform non-sales duties without worrying about loss of earnings.

- Provides stability of income for salesmen, removing the financial uncertainties which can affect performance. *Note*: Certain types of salesmen work best on a straight salary system, but this is very much the exception rather than the rule. Offering such a person the option to take straight salary may be considered. This requires close personal knowledge of the individual. If it's offered, management should reserve the right to change back to the regular company pay plan for any reason in the future. It will also be necessary to keep the salary at a level lower than the potential earnings of an average salesman, to avoid complaints of unfairness.

Disadvantages

- Removes financial incentive.
- Could lead to overpayment of poor salesmen and underpayment of top performers.
- Always the danger of top salesmen being tempted away by a competitor who is able to offer prospects of higher earnings.
- New business opportunities could be missed, because salesmen are not motivated sufficiently to look for orders.
- A higher rate of absenteeism could occur, because salesmen suffer no loss of commission earnings when they are away from work.
- Arguments can occur over differential salary scales, cost of living increases, long service awards.
- Sales expenses are fixed and the company has the same wage bill even if sales go down. Management are then obliged to sack salesmen as the only means of reducing costs.
- Sales performance has to be monitored for a commission plan to be effective. A straight salary plan removes the necessity for this quantitative exercise and is therefore likely to lower efficiency. Managers will also be unable to assess accurately a salesman's performance, leading to inequities in salary scales.

2) Commission only pay plan

Advantages

- The company pays strictly according to sales productivity.
- Maximum financial incentive is provided, offering the biggest 'carrot' to the top salesmen.
- Usually this method attracts only top calibre salesmen because poor salesmen can't survive.
- Company sales expenses become directly variable in tune with sales volume.
- Great flexibility. Commission rates can quickly be adjusted with immediate effect, for example, to correct a stock imbalance or promote a new product.

Disadvantages

- Uncertainty of earnings.
- Danger of salesmen using pressure methods or badly advising customers in order to achieve sales, regardless of damage to goodwill.
- The company has little financial control over the salesmen.
- More difficult for the company to exercise discipline.
- Does not encourage salesmen to be loyal to the company. He's more likely to regard himself as an agent, rather than an employee.
- Difficult to determine the best commission base, i.e. should commission be paid on sales turnover, varied for different product lines, etc.

3) Salary plus commission pay plan

These are the most popular sales pay plans. They combine many of the advantages outlined above, and remove some major disadvantages. The key to a successful salary/commission plan is in the ratio of the split between fixed and variable earnings. This will vary according to the nature of the company business, type of product, and structure of the sales organisation. Ratios within the bands 60/40 to 80/20 fixed/variable earnings are the most effective. Too little 'carrot' can fail to motivate salesmen in certain circumstances, for example if the company wish to promote sales of a product which is traditionally difficult to sell. Alternatively a ratio biased too heavily towards commission can result in the disadvantages listed under the straight commission plan.

The disadvantages of this combination plan are that it's more expensive to administer efficiently. Accurate records have to be kept. Also it will of necessity be more complicated, leading to the possibility of misunderstandings amongst sales staff.

4) Salary plus commission plus bonus or profit sharing

This is perhaps the best form of remuneration for senior

salesmen or sales managers. If the bonus element is to be
made to work, regular estimates of bonus earnings should
be made available. A bonus of between 5 and 15 per cent
of annual earnings is the most popular choice. Some companies pay a bonus on company net profits, but the disadvantage of this system is that the employee receives it late
and has no real indication of what he's likely to earn during the year the bonus is supposed to be acting as a
motivator. One advantage of an effective annual bonus
system, from a company point of view, is that it may deter
a good salesman from leaving, at least until the end of
the year.

Conclusion

The sales pay plan is an essential part of the total motivation 'package' for sales personnel. The various combina-
tions of salary/commission/bonus should ensure a living
wage, but be sufficiently flexible to adjust for variations in
sales performance. Expense reimbursement should be
structured fairly, avoiding the possibility of being looked
upon as an opportunity for additional income.

Today's salesmen tend to take fringe benefits and company car for granted. However, managers could make better use of company benefits by taking the trouble to sell
these to salesmen. For example there are many first class
pension plans which offer good opportunities for salesmen
to build future savings.

Other types of motivator

1)   Sales incentives

Today's managers appreciate the importance of sales incentives as a motivational tool. This is evidenced by the
huge growth of the incentive industry over the past two
decades. Incentives are big business, because it's been
proved time and again that incentives really do work.
Thousands of companies have benefited from the discov-

ery that salesmen respond well to a well planned incentive scheme. More instantly effective than any other motivation tool, properly handled, this device can be the key to sales success. The subject is dealt with at length in subsequent chapters of this book. *This motivates people* ✓ Ⓐ

2) Sales training

The importance of regular training should not be underestimated. Training sessions provide excellent opportunities for skilled managers to motivate salesmen. Effective and interesting sales training meetings or seminars (sometimes inviting interesting guest speakers from outside the company) can be events for salesmen to look forward to. Training in self development should be included in the programme. Most salesmen are keenly interested in developing their personal abilities, and offering this type of training course to promising salesmen can itself be a strong motivator.

3) Company cars

The salesmen's car can be a very emotive factor in his life. It can be used to motivate, but it's more likely to demotivate. The manáger who attempts to motivate by motor car is venturing into a minefield. It's easy to reward a salesman with a better car for improved sales performance, but difficult to take it back when he stops performing. The manager should, if possible, use his influence to ensure that his salesmen are given the most suitable car for the job. He would be wise to stick to a firm policy and avoid deviations which may cause dissent amongst his sales team.

4) Supervision and discipline

Many companies mistakenly believe that salesmen are a unique breed of human being. They imagine that salesmen can work better on their own without supervision and with no-one regularly checking their activities or performance. Nothing could be further from the truth. Salesmen, like everyone else, work better when supervised.

Much depends on the character of the individual. Many naturally gifted salesmen have been spoilt by a negligent management approach. They've been allowed to develop bad habits and become inefficient, thus making future management control more difficult. For example, activities such as report writing and route planning may have become inefficient. It's possible that a salesman who has the most brilliant natural talent needs strong discipline to motivate and develop him in the right direction.

5) Promotion prospects

It's probably impossible to offer every salesmen genuine prospects of promotion. However, an alert manager will pick out the most likely candidates and make use of this opportunity to provide extra motivation.

6) Educational opportunities

Most salesmen are interested in improving their education. Managers should encourage any relevant outside interests or extra-curricular studies by salesmen wishing to improve their education. The best possible way to exploit this as a motivator is to offer to arrange educational visits abroad for salesmen to study companies at work in similar fields.

7) Sales meetings

One of the objectives for management at every sales meeting should be to create opportunities to motivate sales staff. Whatever the main purpose of the meeting, no salesman should be allowed to leave until an attempt has been made to (a) keep him motivated, (b) arouse enough enthusiasm to motivate him at least until the next meeting, (c) remove any factors causing demotivation.

8) Leadership

Most managers have qualities of leadership which is

partly why they were selected for the job. Leadership is a powerful motivator. Often in a busy work schedule managers don't pay enough attention to developing this aspect of their own ability, which could be of benefit to their salesmen. Sometimes it's simply a matter of spending more time in the field with the salesmen to lead and therefore motivate by example.

9) Social events

Any social gathering with salesmen or salesmen and wives, should be a happy, relaxed occasion. Parties, informal dinners, company outings can all provide opportunities for a manager to get to know his salesmen better. Such occasions can also be used to enlist the support and understanding of salesmen's wives. They sometimes take a keen interest in their husbands' work, and are more likely to be understanding during times when pressure of work or late meetings keep him away from home.

Sales motivation audit

Incentives can only be made to work effectively when the rest of the organisation is operating efficiently. A sales audit can be a useful exercise. It provides a check on those matters which may affect the morale and motivation of the salesmen. The manager can then take steps to correct areas of weakness, before introducing regular sales incentives.

SALES AUDIT

Factors affecting efficiency, morale and motivation	Good	Fair	Poor	Action Plan
1 Do all salesmen have clear job descriptions?				
2 Are sales targets clearly defined and quantified?				
3 Are salesmen promptly made aware of changes in company policy?				
4 Does the sales department enjoy good relations and co-operation from other departments?				
5 Is the sales manager a good leader and motivator?				
6 Do the salesmen receive regular sales training and product instruction?				
7 Is the managing director 'sales minded'?				
8 Do salesmen receive constructive support in the field from their manager?				
9 Are salesmen encouraged in the process of self development?				
10 Has the sales manager been professionally trained in the skills of sales management?				

Factors affecting efficiency, morale and motivation	Good	Fair	Poor	Action Plan
11 Does the sales manager keep in close communication with his salesmen?				
12 Does the sales manager lead by example, or sit behind a desk most of the time?				
13 Is sales activity efficiently monitored?				
14 Is positive corrective action taken to improve performance in fall down areas?				
15 Are salesmen given targets for number of effective sales calls which they are expected to make?				
16 If call rate falls below target are salesmen allowed to lapse?				
17 Are the salesmen enthusiastic and well motivated?				
18 How is their attendance record compared to other staff?				
19 Are the salesmen regarded with respect by other staff for doing a professional job?				
20 Estimate the level of job satisfaction demonstrated by the sales force				
21 What appears to be the general attitude to the job by members of the sales force?				
22 Are salesmen regularly assessed and graded for capability by the sales manager?				
23 Is their assessment and grading discussed with each individual?				
24 Does the company management feel that salesmen work hard with enough determination?				

Factors affecting efficiency, morale and motivation	Good	Fair	Poor	Action Plan
25 Do they seek new business with enthusiasm?				
26 How is their product knowledge?				
27 Do they ever make suggestions and contribute ideas for improving sales?				
28 Do managers have regular meetings with salesmen, allowing full two way participation?				
29 Does the managing director talk regularly to salesmen?				
30 Are salesmen kept up to date with information through sales bulletins or newsletter?				
31 Are memos from salesmen to head office answered promptly and positively?				
32 Has the sales call rate shown an improving trend over the last 12 months?				
33 Are salesmen increasing profitable sales at a satisfactory rate?				
34 Is a regular and accurate analysis of weekly sales produced and distributed to salesmen?				
35 How many regular customers have been lost in the 12 months?				
36 Are salesmen provided with professional sales literature and demonstration kits?				
37 Do salesmen participate at all in budgeting?				
38 Do salesmen get active support from head office to help them service key accounts?				

Factors affecting efficiency, morale and motivation	Good	Fair	Poor	Action Plan
39 Has the sales force remuneration system been reviewed in the past year?				
40 Is the commission element in salesmen's earnings big enough to act as an incentive?				
41 Is there a limit on salesmen's earnings?				
42 Is the sales commission system sales and profit related?				
43 Are regular sales contests operated?				
44 Has any recent attempt been made to study and remove possible disincentives?				
45 Has the sales manager received formal training in motivation techniques?				
46 What is the usual response to recruitment advertising for company salesmen?				

A brief assessment of these factors will provide managers with a useful indicator of motivational efficiency. Obviously, it would be unwise for a manager to plan any form of incentive programme without first ensuring at least a fair standard from an audit of the sales organisation.

Efficient sales management, combined with proper use of motivational skills. This can produce positive improvements, and make the difference between success and failure for a product, a company, or salesman.

The role of incentives in sales management

A well planned, efficiently run sales incentive is the surest and most immediately effective way to motivate salesmen towards improving sales performance. Essentially, sales incentives, usually designed in the form of contests, have three requirements:

1 To motivate the sales force to expend greater efforts and improve sales productivity.
2 The extra effort must be worthwhile in terms of reward for the sales force and the company.
3 It must encourage the sales force to become more efficient, and therefore more productive in the future.

There can be many other benefits resulting from a good sales incentive. It can improve sales force morale, lead to improved job satisfaction, stimulate interest, add excitement, introduce a 'fun' element to a job routine. Develop latent ability, foster pride in the job, promote friendly competition, improve product knowledge, benefit communications. Team sales incentive contests in larger companies can add impetus to field training, encourage *esprit de corps* and develop a sense of group responsibility. The flexibility of sales incentives is one of the main attractions of this motivational tool.

Motivation has become a modern science, resulting in the rapid expansion of incentive marketing as an industry. Merchandise awards, gift vouchers, prize point schemes, holidays, sport, education, entertainment, are typical of the desirable prizes used to excite ambitious salesmen. The salesmen are the front line troops. They virtually hold the key to success or failure. But incentives don't work by themselves. Too many managers allow incentive failures, through poor planning, weak promotion, lack of interest, or simply not taking enough time to see the job through efficiently.

The manager who introduces a successful incentive has to make time to plan it carefully, imaginatively, and in detail. He also has to sell it to his salesmen. Then he has to supervise it efficiently and stimulate interest by regularly promoting and publicising the incentive right through the period of a campaign.

How to design, plan and promote an effective sales incentive campaign

An incentive is best used as a short term stimulant to a sales activity. Regular use of incentives, following a predetermined programme, makes good motivational sense. However, an element of suprise should always be maintained. Incentives should never be predictable, as this could lead to the possibility of manipulation by a shrewd salesman. For example, he could hold back orders in anticipation, or temporarily reduce his effort on a particular product, in the hope that the harassed sales manager will choose that product for his next incentive campaign.

Questions to be raised at the planning stage are as follows:

1   What is the objective?
2   What type of competition? For example, it might take the form of a team sales contest. Alternatively, the salesman may be challenged to better his previous individual performance.
3   What will it be called? It may help to focus attention and promote the incentive if a topical, imaginative title is used. The incentive may be designed to link in with an existing customer promotion or television commercial. For example, a 'superdeal' car promotion for customers, could run concurrently with a 'superdeal' incentive promotion for salesmen. Even the best incentive still needs to be promoted to the participants. The importance of retaining interest and 'keeping the pressure on' is often neglected by managers. They make the mistake of thinking that having announced an imaginative incentive campaign with a really attractive prize award they can then forget about it until it ends. This can lead to a falling off of interest by the salesmen in the early stages, resulting in loss of impact and effectiveness.
4   How long should incentives last? Incentives are best used to provide a short sharp boost to sales activity. A six-week period is considered the optimum for a sales incentive campaign to run, plus a week before and after to announce and launch the campaign, then scrutinise results and make the award to winners. The length of time an incentive should run depends on a variety of circumstances. For example, it may be decided to give a short boost to sales of a product to compensate for a seasonal fall off in sales. On the other hand, a new product launch may need a longer period of extra sales effort to get the product properly 'off the ground'. A sales incentive campaign may also be linked with an advertising campaign. This is particularly suitable for consumer products, to take advantage of maximum impact during peak promotion periods.

From the beginning, the regular promotion of an incentive campaign should be carefully planned. Initial literature should be as good as the budget allows. The company advertising agent can assist in producing attractive literature. He will know 'tricks of the trade' to reduce printing costs, and possible use of previous artwork can be considered. Letters, sales bulletins (specially designed to reflect the theme of the campaign) posters and novelty gifts, can all be used regularly throughout the campaign period. Up to date information showing results via a 'leader board' or newsletter, is also a vital part of adding impetus to the promotion of the incentive. For example, if a holiday abroad is the star prize, post cards could carry a message such as 'wish you were here'. This way, a great deal of interest can be created, including incentivising of the salesman's family. A trip aboard 'Concorde' promotion may include a model of the plane given to every salesmen or a booklet describing the building of the plane. A visit to a world cup football match could be preceded by novelty gifts carrying the world cup motif. A Wimbledon tennis prize could be given extra impact by issuing T-shirts with 'anyone for tennis?' logo and so on.

Typical sales incentives

'Treasure Island' was the theme for a successful incentive campaign operated by a well-known cosmetics manufacturer. During the course of the campaign the 150 participants (most sales girls) were all given a key to a 'treasure chest'. Achieving stage 1 of the contest enabled them to open the chest and choose an item of jewellery as a prize. The next key for stage 2 opened another chest, culminating in the last key which opened a chest containing tickets for two to an island in the sun. Travel brochures (at no cost) were sent to the sales girls' homes to involve all the family in the dream of winning and to encourage their own contestant. The scheme was announced at a sales conference held at a luxury hotel. Every opportunity was taken to add excitement and 'showmanship' to the incentive promotion.

'Autumn Gold' was the title for an incentive campaign operated by a car distributor. The prizes offered to the successful salesmen in this promotion were gold Krugerrands. The objective was to increase sales on slow moving stock of new and used cars. 'Gold points' were allocated to selected stock and salesmen were awarded their first Krugerrand once the individual points total had achieved a predetermined total. A leader board, constantly updated, showed weekly results which were issued to various branches. This introduced a competitive element into the incentive promotion. All salesmen had an equal opportunity of scoring points and winning prizes. Because the incentive concentrated on stock vehicles the salesmen were spurred on to act quickly before anyone else sold the cars. Regular sales bulletins on 'Impakt' stationery carried good humoured messages to the sales force. The campaign ran for twelve weeks. This was rather longer than the company had planned. It was extended from an original eight-week period to include extra vehicles in the successful promotion.

Incentive marketing specialists will of course design, organise, and promote a whole range of incentive prizes. Sales managers can make use of these excellent services. However, it's essential that they retain control and flexibility. It may be necessary to make a rapid change, or switch emphasis from one product to another. Prompt action is the only way to handle this in order to maintain momentum. A stand-by promotion kit can be prepared for such an emergency.

When to use incentives

Ideas for using sales incentives are detailed in a later chapter. Timing is vitally important. It's best to prepare an outline programme well in advance. Then incentives can be slotted in at short notice throughout the year, retaining an element of surprise.

Waiting until a problem arises, then hoping that an incentive scheme will perform miracles isn't really an effective way to operate. Employing incentives to add further success to a sales drive by keeping the momentum going, can often achieve more satisfactory and cost effective results.

Incentive travel the prime motivator?

The following overview of the incentive business discusses particularly the growing role of travel in the incentive industry and is taken from articles which have appeared in *Sales and Marketing Management* magazine.

'MOTIVATE SALES TEAMS WITH TRAVEL (1980)

Travel writer Peter Eadie who has visited many travel incentive destinations throughout the world in the past year, highlights some of the places he has visited and gives case histories of companies which have used travel to motivate their sales teams, to such an extent that in one case sales doubled in a three-month period.

Until quite recently, a company's concept of a reward to employees was a gold watch after 50 years of hard work and that was it. But as employers became more enlightened, awards began to take the form of TV sets, Hi-Fi equipment and other luxury incentives. Then the Americans pioneered the holiday incentive. Employers were soon to find that, for encouraging greater sales effort, better production and higher efficiency, this was the best motivator. And within two decades of its innovation, businesses were spending a billion dollars per annum on incentive travel.

It caught on in Britain and developed particularly during the period when employers were unable to motivate or reward staff by wage increases because they were frozen to a low percentage level. Like many good opportunities, this form of award was in some cases abused in the United States. Accordingly, methods of taxing companies and individuals there, have now been established for this form of fringe benefit. So far, the Inland Revenue here have not imposed any set regulations. It has been left up to companies to act responsibly and for individual tax inspectors to assess each situation on its own merit. But this may soon change.

There is now a growing tendency to combine incentive holidays with one or two mornings of conference meetings. This is a sensible development which puts the event on a better business footing from a tax standpoint. It also enables the organisation to look back over the past year's trading in convivial circumstances and to develop schemes to reach new profit targets at a time when the benefits of past hard work are being enjoyed most.

Incentive travel schemes for sales executives and their wives are now usually paid for out of additional profits accruing from set targets, i.e. from extra earnings, not current earnings.

In planning travel incentive schemes one has first to define clearly the objective, what project requires pushing and who can be motivated to carry this out most successfully. Then the target period requires to be set. One needs to bear in mind that a too long period makes maintaining the original impetus difficult. Too short a time also has its pitfalls. A period of six to nine months is usually the right length of time for a promotion within a medium size company.

Having said that, there was an interesting case not long ago when the Marketing Director of an American-owned Transinternational Life Insurance Company turned to his sales force in September and said that sales had to be doubled by the end of the year. If they met with success he promised they would all meet with their wives in the New Year at the Southampton Princess Hotel in Bermuda and added that both achievers and non-achievers would be invited but non-achievers would have to pay 50% of the cost of bringing their wives if they wished to come along too. Company sales were doubled in the last three months.

The next decision is which destination and what type of holiday to select. It should be one that the executive and his wife have little chance of affording out of earned income.

In planning the reward, estimate how many people are likely to qualify and then assess the hobbies of the competitors, also remembering their wives. This will help you develop the outline of the holiday, including special features which you believe would be of interest.

Not long ago Scottish and Newcastle Breweries produced an incentive trip of enormous interest appeal. The reward included a holiday in Argentina and also tickets to the key games in the World Soccer Finals. Its appeal led to great effort which benefited the breweries very substantially. It was a good choice because it motivated the type of person they wanted to reach, particularly as Scotland was participating in the matches.

The hotel which is selected should be of high quality in a good area of whatever destination you finally decide on. Hotels like the Grand Verdala or Dragonara in Malta, which are represented by Maxhotels at Seaford or the Southampton Princess or Hamilton Princess represented by Nick Lawson Limited in London or the Balaia in the Algarve, represented by Penta Hotels at Ascot or Gleneagles in Scotland. These are just some suggestions in a field rich in choice.

In the case of incentives for employers or dealers, the recognition of achievement should be maximised. The presentation of awards should be made an occasion, best carried out at a banquet. Awards should be presented by someone at the highest level in the company or by a celebrity. Finally, for the benefit of company publicity, aim to get good media coverage. Mention of achievements by individuals is always of interest to local newspapers, and to trade and institute journals.

The next important item is to give each winner a presentation pack with a letter of congratulation from the chairman, schedule of activities with times, air tickets, excursion passes, invitation cards to gala functions and so on. At one recent function in Malta the company provided every winner with a copy of the *Blue Guide to Malta* (published by Ernest Benn Limited) because they thought that it would assist them with sightseeing and would also serve as a memento of the occasion.

The most attractive incentive areas have usually been developed with a certain amount of care and imagination and seldom deteriorate of their own accord. However, political changes, vogue, currency exchange rates and alteration in transport patterns do create change. Hence new areas are becoming available all the time.

The lowering of long haul fares generally has made exotic destinations more accessible. For example, Nairobi/

return is on offer with airfares as low as £250 if booked sufficiently far in advance. Both British Airways and Kenya Airways fly direct from Heathrow. For futher information on exotic destinations out of the UK, a good contact is Mike Cox, British Airways Incentive Travel Executive at West London Terminal. Kenya is only an overnight flight and offers two great attractions – wildlife safaris through its magnificent game parks, combined with first-class hotels by magnificent beaches at the time of the year when the winter is bleak at home.

The Caribbean is still one of the most popular long haul destinations and probably will remain so for some time. Similar scenic beauty is to be found in Mauritius, Réunion and the Seychelles in the Indian Ocean. To Réunion, Air France provide the largest number of scheduled flights and for incentive ideas it is well worth looking through the excellent Air France Holidays brochure, or contacting them at 18 Burton Place, London for ideas.

Air Mauritius, the national carrier and some twelve other airlines fly into Mauritius. And the Meridien, Trou-aux-Biches, Le Morne Brabant and other luxury hotels are represented by the Mauritius Hotels Group at 30 Old Bond Street, London.

In the Far East, Singapore is interesting and now ranks as one of the cleanest cities in the world. For a taste of the best of the old colonial world, then choose Raffles where guests enjoy their thinly-diced cucumber sandwiches for tea and the Singapore Sling, a cocktail which one of their barmen invented. Singapore Airlines have created a reputation for good service and now fly Concorde to this destination. Bali is an enchanting Far East venue with beautiful beaches, fascinating Hindu temples and dancing. Its only problem is the limitation in numbers of luxury class hotels.'

'TRAVEL – TOMORROW'S PRIME MOTIVATOR (1981)

The use of incentive programmes to motivate sales forces is becoming an increasingly acceptable business practice in the UK. However, not too long ago the story was very different. Incentives, dealer loaders and other 'perks' were very much frowned upon by large sections of both the business community and public opinion.

europe

But with the effects of the recession biting deep into the nation's profits, more and more companies are turning to incentives to help their sales forces increase sales, turnover and market share.

During the past decade or so the incentives business has boomed, with E.F. Macdonald and Maritz, both offshoots of giant American parents, leading the field.

According to Christian Petersen, a director of the Kingsland Lloyd Petersen sales promotion consultancy and author of *Sales Promotion in Action* (Associated Business Press, 1979) around £45 million is spent every year on motivating Britain's sales forces. It's only an estimate, of course, but then true figures concerning promotional and motivational activity are extremely difficult or simply impossible to obtain.

Yet by no means are all sales personnel in this country offered incentive schemes, so the true value of the incentive market potential must be much higher than Petersen's figure, probably in the region of £100 million-plus – and growing.

The most common form sales motivation takes is the simple catalogue scheme with a points system.

Sales staff are awarded points and bonuses for reaching set targets. The points, awards, or whatever, can be exchanged for items available in the catalogue supplied by the incentive house. More sophisticated operations will have an incentive theme, such as 'The Great Bread Race', and a catalogue specially designed for the programme. But in essence the theory and the practice are the same.

The double problem the incentive and motivation houses have to face is that of selling the idea of the scheme to their sales personnel and at the same time providing a sufficiently exciting end target. The most common solution is travel.

John Mulford, managing director of E.F. Macdonald in London, maintains that it is the promise of travel which is the prime motivator. Sales personnel work harder when they know that they might achieve a trip to some sunny isle if they reach a particular set target. And yet when it comes to selecting the merchandise awards during the course of an incentive programme, more than 90% of participants opt not for travel but for 'something for the house' instead. Nevertheless, travel is still considered to be a prime motivator.

To see why, one can examine just how an increasingly typical British incentive programme actually works.

First, the sales force are introduced to the programme at a sales conference or briefing held at a five-star hotel, rather than at the company's own premises. In fact the hotel itself, in London or wherever, will have become the first incentive travel destination in the total package.

The sales force are excited about being at an expensive hotel and so are more receptive to the programme proposition offering them pots, pans, furniture and clocks in return for extra effort. The sales force begin to compete for points based on the programme's specific theme.

Then, some months later, the high-flyers, probably the top 50%, are invited to attend, with their spouses, a two or three-day conference in Paris. Of course, the conference is important, but equally so is the fact that would-be delegates were informed of the intended trip some weeks in advance and worked extra hard to earn a place on it.

At the Paris conference the final details of the incentive programme are revealed. At the end of a second set period a selection of the very best sales personnel will be sent, with their spouses, to, for example, the Bahamas or Singapore for a week, which will include a short conference or sales meeting.

Naturally enough, the trip to a sunnier clime will be used by the company to introduce the next incentive programme. The lucky top 'delegates' will return home and their example will provide an added stimulus to their colleagues.

It is important to note that incentive travel is rarely used entirely on its own to motivate sales forces; almost without exception it is tied in with a merchandise-based programme. This balance is reflected each year at the Incentive Marketing and Sales Promotion Exhibition at Brighton.

When the exhibition opens at the Metropole on 26th April the vast majority of the stands will be showing merchandise of all sorts although incorporated with the show there will be displays from the Costa del Sol, the Bahamas, Portugal, British West Indies Airlines, and others.

With the advent of cheaper air fares, incentive travel has grown at a phenomenal rate, not only in Britain but also in other European countries, such as Italy and Spain. One might be excused for thinking that Spain's only contribution to incentive travel was in offering venues and locations, but this is simply not the case. Today's Spanish sales representatives are even more likely to find themselves on an incentive trip than their British counterparts!

In 1981, however, the growth rate of incentive travel in Britain did level off quite considerably. 'Because of the economic recession, some companies definitely cut back their budgets', says David Preece of Conference and Incentive Directions; 'but prospects for 1982 and beyond look very good indeed'.

Preece supports the view that in some ways the recession may actually be helping the incentive travel business. 'New clients are hard to come by for many companies,' he explains, 'and more and more of them are having to get their sales forces to go out and get new business, so there is a considerable increase in incentive activity.'

Even so, Preece points out that it is the companies with industrial clients which are taking up the running again; those with trading relationships with retail outlets are, as he puts it, 'less inclined to shell out money.'

Incentive destinations can be divided into two main types, long-haul and short-haul, with medium-haul as a subdivision. Generally, short-haul and domestic mean short stays of two or three days in London, Amsterdam or Paris, while long- and medium-haul destinations include jet-lag and longer stays in Singapore, Barbados or Bali.

It might seem strange to us here in Britain, but London was considered as a top 'first-time-out' long- or medium-haul destination for American incentive programmes a few years ago.

Over the past couple of years the strong pound, reputedly grubby and outrageously expensive hotels and the fact that most incentivised sales forces had visited the UK already meant that London gave way to other European destinations.

Now, with more American companies taking up the incentive travel concept, London may soon be coming back into its own.

But where are British incentive programmes going? 'For short-haul, North Africa, particularly Tunisia, has become more popular than Mallorca and the South of France for the time being', says David Preece. 'Top of the list among long-haul destinations are Hong Kong and the USA.'

In other words, incentive travel 'flavours of the mouth' tend to follow closely the trends set by consumer tourist travel. Not long ago it was the Bahamas and Trinidad and, of course, Amsterdam.

What of the future? Who knows? With China becoming easier to visit, anything could happen.

But one thing is certain. With more and more companies learning the important marketing equation that incentive and conference travel is virtually cost-free because the extra profits derived from sales always outweigh the programme expense, incentive travel is going to grow and grow.'

Part II
Sales Incentives
in Action

Sales incentive ideas

'Your own resolution to succeed, is more important than any one thing' (Lincoln)

A sales manager should continually stimulate and encourage his salesmen's natural competitive instincts. The vital enthusiasm essential to successful selling needs to be constantly fuelled by imaginative and understanding management. Understanding the importance of the salesman's role, the ups and downs of a salesman's life, and recognising his emotional drives, is a part of creative sales management.

A sales contest should enthuse, motivate and encourage all participants, and it should be fun. The carefully designed and planned contest should motivate equally the star performers and the newcomers or average performers.

Competitive selling really works, when salesmen can be shown fair opportunities of winning by achieving realistic sales targets.

The following pages contain incentive ideas, many of which have been drawn from practical, successful experience in a variety of companies. The most popular subjects show a number of incentives, and their cost is indicated as follows: economy (£), medium price (££), expensive (£££), variable (£±).

Objectives

The objectives of a sales incentive scheme will vary according to requirements. Changing market situations will demand many different approaches which will test the imagination of the sales manager. For example, increasing sales may not be an appropriate objective if the company is faced with production problems. Likewise, increasing profit could conflict with company policy if that policy were to increase market share.

Typical objectives which can form the basis of a sales incentive campaign are:

1   Increase sales.
2   Increase profit.
3   Improve sales efficiency.
4   Encourage sales teamwork.
5   Obtain customer recommendations.
6   Stimulate new sales ideas.
7   Test product knowledge.
8   Increase new business prospecting.
9   Launch a new product.
10 Improve customer relations.
11 Promote special products or services.
12 Boost salesmen's morale.

Ideas taken from practical applications of incentive schemes are classified according to objective in the following pages.

1) Increase Sales

(a)

'A trip on the greatest ship in the world – QE2. Enjoy the luxury, the style, the thrills of a sea voyage. Relax in the comfort of a first class cabin. Dine in the first class restaurant and enjoy five star catering. Spend your time sight-seeing from the decks and exploring the ship – longer than three football pitches and thirteen decks high! Tingle with excitement as she steams out of port. Find out for yourself the magic of QE2. Share in the glorious history and great maritime traditions. Remember forever. Truly, the experience of a lifetime.'

This is a wonderful idea for a prize which lends itself to a whole range of sales incentives contests.

The following notes are taken from material used in a number of sales incentive campaigns, featuring a QE2 cruise as the prize.

Suggested campaign titles

'Crest of a Wave'/'Anchors Away'/'Sail Time'

This is a sales incentive which will really motivate all the sales team to get out selling. It's a contest they'll all want to win. The prize is original, low cost, and lends itself to so many imaginative ideas which can be used to stimulate and maintain interest during the campaign period.

Requirements

Prestige illustrated folders overprinted with the company name. The folders describe all the details of the sales incentive campaign and QE2 trip. (Cunard produce very attractive colour brochures advertising QE2. These can be obtained from Cunard in London or Southampton.) Presentation and launch material with further details of the sales contest, including sales targets and a personal message from the managing director. A colour slide presentation of the QE2 on a cruise, for use at sales meetings. News bulletins issued regularly, carrying the campaign message and including up to date progress. An attractive poster publicising the results of the contest and displaying a merit table or leader board.

Interesting and attractive QE2 novelty gifts mailed to the homes of the participants, sent out at regular intervals during the period of the campaign. (Cunard can supply.) The prize tickets can be purchased through selected travel agents. (Cunard will advise.)

Cost category £

This is a surprisingly low cost incentive which can produce most effective results.

Alternative QE2 prize

A one week cruise to New York on QE2/fly back British Airways. The advantage of this is that if a number of winners are involved it could be convenient for the company to organise a two stage trip, i.e. half the party cruise out and fly back and the other half fly out and cruise back a week later.

Cost category ££

(b)

'Men have a touchstone whereby to try gold, but gold is the touchstone whereby to try men' (Thomas Fuller)

The gold theme is an ideal subject for a number of sales incentives. It lends itself to imaginative promotional material. It has a universal appeal to salesmen of all ages and interests. A desirable, powerful motivator. History has proof of that! Successful sales incentives have featured gold shares or gold coins. The gold shares idea is more difficult for a company to administer, but a good bank manager can take care of the share acquisitions or purchase of Krugerrands.

This sales incentive campaign can be launched at a sales meeting, or by direct mail to the salesmen. Choose the targets, make them fair and achievable, then look forward to a sales increase.

Suggested campaign titles

'Gold Rush'/'Go for Gold'/'Golden Opportunity'

Prize

Shares in a gold mine, or gold Krugerrands. This sales incentive contains all the elements that make a good contest – simplicity, desirability, excitement, interest, reward. Plus a bonus if the shares or coins increase in value after the award to the winning salesman. Of course, there's no guarantee that they will appreciate in value and it's possible they'll even decrease. However, on one occasion this contest was run, two winning salesmen found their shares increased by around 250 per cent inside twelve months. The effect was to focus attention on the sales drive long after the prizes had been awarded, not to mention the boost in morale of two very happy salesmen!

The prize is original and the campaign publicity material can be designed for maximum impact on the sales team

Requirements

Shares in a gold mine purchased in the name of the winning salesman. The shares will be acquired on the recommendation of a professional stockbroker at the time the contest ends. (Alternatively, purchase of coins at market rate.) Illustrated folders printed with company name, giving details about the incentive campaign and describing how it works.

Weekly news bulletins carrying the campaign message and reporting up to date results of the contest. An original poster illustrating a facsimile of a Gold Share Certificate or Krugerrand, much enlarged. Low cost gimmick gifts to salesmen during the campaign (e.g. guide to stocks and shares, imitation gold dust from the mine, gold plated key ring.)

Cost category ££

(c)

A very low cost, but nonetheless effective spur to the competitive instincts of salesmen. Each month, the salesman who achieves the best performance has his name inscribed on a challenge trophy, kept in a prominent position in the sales manager's office. (Care must be taken to ensure the measurement of sales performance is based on a system approved by the company and accepted as fair by the salesmen.) At the end of the year, the salesman who wins the most 'Salesmen of the Month' awards keeps the trophy. In the event of a tie, the salesman with the best performance in the thirteenth month wins the trophy. It is recommended that the 'Salesman of the Month' award is announced each month at a sales meeting. Periodically, invite top executives from the company to present the award; it further enhances the value to the winning salesman, in terms of recognition and prestige.

Suggested campaign titles

'Salesmen of the Month Award'/'Merit Award for Sales Excellence'/'Sales Performance Award'

Prize

A challenge cup, a shield, or an engraved plaque. In terms of value for money, this can be the most effective piece of furniture ever to grace the sales manager's office.

This incentive brings out the competitive instincts of salesmen. It has the advantages of working over a long period, at low cost.

Requirements

Cup, shield or plaque suitable for engraving. Letters for distribution to salesmen attractively designed and announcing the introduction of the award. Monthly news bulletins to announce results and carry details of the next monthly sales target. Engraving of winners' names *promptly* on the trophy.

Cost category £

2) Increase Profits

(a) A day out

There are obvious dangers in motivating salesmen too strongly towards increasing profit. It depends on the type of product and the business relationship between salesman and buyer. For example, a salesman may be acting on behalf of a manufacturer, selling widgets to wholesale stockists. He may be tempted to pressure the customer into overstocking widgets, thus jeopardising future business relationships, and killing all demand for widgets for months after the contest! Alternatively, a salesman selling a highly technical scatter system to computer users will most likely need to improve his negotiating skills if he wishes to increase profitability, but he could be influenced into recommending a scatter system above the customer's level of needs.

Whatever the product or type of business, it will be necessary for management to control with care the activities of salesmen who are extra-profit motivated. However, that is not to say that incentives aimed at increasing profit should not be attempted. In fact, this is probably the most popular objective for sales incentive contests.

A successful profit incentive shouldn't cost anything. The financial cost of the incentive is merely a part of the added total contribuition. Professional salesmen should be motivated to make an extra contribution and given the opportunity of really high earnings. Unfortunately, too many companies adopt the outdated philosophy that salesmen's earnings should be restricted. If the extra profit potential can be translated into a real sales motivator, then it ensures that more sales, or more profitable sales opportunities are never neglected.

What's wrong with making money? What's a salesman for? With all the fancy titles bandied about these days, one suspects there is an aversion to the title of salesman: 'account executive', 'negotiator', 'marketing assistant', 'technical representative', 'consultant' to name but a few of the salesman's pseudonyms. Selling is a job to be proud of, not ashamed of, so why disguise the name? Salesmen are in the selling business to make money. Making money for the company secures the future of every employee, from the managing director to the shop floor and office worker.

The following incentives focus on the most important part of a salesman's job – making money!

'It is a Socialist idea that making profits is a vice. I consider that the real vice is making losses'

(Winston Churchill)

Example: horse racing

Suggested campaign titles

'First past the post'/'Every one a winner'/'The big race'

Prize

A day out for two at the races, according to season. Royal Ascot, Epsom Derby or Grand National (with spending money).The day begins with lunch at a top class restaurant, then the winning couple are chauffeur driven to the races. First class tickets for the enclosure will enable them to relax and enjoy the excitement, pleasures, and profits (?) of this Sport of Kings! Your winning salesman doesn't have to be a gambler. He can still enjoy a thoroughly entertaining day and savour the excitement and thrills of big race day.

Requirements

Trip for two to Royal Ascot, Epsom Derby or Grand National, including a five course lunch with champagne in a first class restaurant. Spending money. Attractive brochure, advertising and promoting the sales incentive campaign to your sales staff. Chauffeur driven car/coach from appropriate pick-up points (London for Ascot or

Epsom, Liverpool or Manchester for Grand National).
Presentation and launch material with further details of
the contest, including your sales targets and personal
message. Design, print and distribution of weekly news
bulletins to the participants. A novel 'horse race' competition during the campaign to stimulate interest and focus
attention on the objective. Include betting slips from a
well known bookmaker. Award certificate congratulating
the winner on achieving success in the profit incentive
campaign.

Cost category ££

(b) Premium bonds

A well run competition will often encourage a salesman, through pride and personal gain, to stretch his effort, and therefore, his sales, to a new high level.

Campaign titles

'Premium Bond Jackpot'/'Ernie Money'/'Premium Sales Bonds'

Prize

Premium Bonds.

Here is a sales competition full of interest, full of fun, and full of opportunity for the profit conscious salesman. Premium Savings Bonds have become an established national favourite, popular as an investment gamble and as a gift for adults and children. With prizes each month up to £250,000 there is tremendous scope to promote the competition to your salesmen and generate excitement about winning. Bond prizes are free of income tax and capital gains tax. You can offer bonds from £5 up to £10,000 depending on your budget, or the urgency to increase your profit! Either way, Premium Savings Bonds can work for you and win again and again for your most profitable salesman.

Requirements

Premium Bonds to the value of your choice, for presentation to the winning salesman. Leaflet overprinted with your company name, announcing details, launch dates, contest rules, etc. Attractive, humorous newsletters to announce results and carry your name and a regular message to the participants. ('Impakt' letterheads.) Poster featuring reprint of monthly news items reported in national press, announcing 'Ernie' winners.

Cost category £±

(c) Cash

'But it is pretty to see what money will do'
                                    (Samuel Pepys)

A 'money tree' provides the basis for this simple cash incentive. Profit targets are set, the amount of cash prizes determined, and allocated according to how many 'money leaves' are required on the tree. Each leaf is numbered, and salesmen reaching predetermined profit objectives, are entitled to pick a leaf from the tree. Numbers on the leaves match up to cash values listed on a cash bonus list. The contest continues until all the leaves are picked from the tree or until the closing date of the contest is reached. The first salesmen to achieve targets, will have the best chance of winning the biggest cash prizes.

Suggested campaign titles

'Profit Grows'/'Money Tree'/'Green Pounds'

Prize

Cash.

Requirements

Money tree – this can be a suitable real tree obtained from a local nursery. Alternatively, an artificial tree can be found in many florists or large department stores. Preprinted list of leaf numbers for you to insert your own values of cash prizes. Leaflets overprinted with your company name, announcing details, launch dates, rules, etc. of the sales incentive contest. Attractive, humorous newsletters to announce results and carry your name and a weekly message to the participants.

Cost category £±

3) Improve Sales Efficiency

'You can't sell if you don't tell.'

There are only two possibilities for a good salesman with a saleable product to increase his sales: visit more customers and visit customers more!

An efficient salesman should prepare his sales material and complete 'unproductive' tasks only at times when it isn't possible to visit customers. Productive selling time is the efficiency indicator. Some salesmen spend only about 10 per cent of the available selling time actually talking to customers in a face to face situation. They need to be encouraged to make more calls by better time planning and more skilful interview techniques. They need to be encouraged to exercise that self discipline, which can make all the difference between efficient selling and the unprofitable alternatives.

The main objective of this sales incentive campaign is to increase the number of effective sales calls by each salesman through improved time planning. Measuring the actual increase in the number of effective sales calls can be complicated, time consuming for the manager, and sometimes unfair to the salesman. We suggest that in this competition, any salesman who improves his call rate by 20 per cent or over, earns himself a chance to draw for the valuable prizes.

Suggested campaign titles

'Time Plan'/'Winning Time'/'Now is the time'

Prizes

A fine antique wall clock or a superb gold wristwatch (lady's or gentleman's) or a digital clock radio. A most desirable timepiece for your salesman to own.

Requirements

Antique clock/wristwatch/clock radio displayed at launch meeting). An attractive folder bearing your company name and spelling out the details of the sales incentive campaign, including contest rules, etc. Two records (single) sent to salesmen during campaign (e.g. 'Now is the time to get things right'. 'Time Flies') with appropriate message included. Weekly news bulletin carrying the campaign message and up to date results. Posters for use at launch and presentation meetings.

Cost category ££

4) Encourage Sales Teamwork

Every football manager knows that you can have brilliant individuals but still not have a good team. Selling is such an individual profession, it's sometimes difficult to build a successful sales team. But often it's necessary. Occasions can arise when you need a united effort. When the star performers must combine and co-operate for the sake of the company. Perhaps a re-organisation or a take-over, or a special sales drive demands it. Be ready with a team incentive and be prepared to switch it on to encourage your sales team to work closely together as one efficient unit.

Suggested campaign titles

'The Winning Team'/'Team Spirit'/'Cup Winners'

Prize

A day out for the winning team, to a football cup tie or international match. The winning team can be treated to a complete day out, purchased from one of the leading specialists in sporting entertainment. Enjoyable, even for the less enthusiastic football fans. (Or use the obvious alternatives of cricket or rugby.)

Requirements

Advance purchase of appropriate number of tickets. (A snag if the contest is to be paid for out of extra sales, which may not achieve the necessary target.) Use old football programmes to create interest with promotional literature. (Football clubs will usually supply these without charge, or for a small donation to club funds.) Football novelty gifts can be distributed to all participants during the period of the campaign, to focus attention and interest in the competition. Sales meetings can encourage friendly team rivalry by including a short football quiz between teams, interspersed with product knowledge questions.

A further idea to keep the momentum going is a weekly football pools contest. Team members are included in a weekly 'Treble Chance' draw with a set number of entries apportioned according to which team is in the lead each week. Photographs of team members superimposed in a cartoon type 'football team' can also be effective.

Cost category ££

5) Obtain Customer Recommendations

(a)

'A satisfied customer can become the finest, cheapest, most effective salesman you never *employed. A satisfied customer can be your best friend.*

A satisfied customer is indispensable.

A satisfied customer deserves the best possible service and attention that you can give.

If you're absolutely sure he's satisfied, you can ask him to recommend you to a friend. Then you may have another customer. Then you have to work twice as hard to keep them both satisfied. But it's the most satisfying way for you to do business.'

Of all the ways a salesman has of getting business, the easiest and the cheapest must be through customer recommendations. Too often, they omit to ask the question which most satisfied customers would be only too pleased to help with: 'Can you recommend me to anyone else who may be interested in my company's products?' The links in this golden opportunity chain are limitless, starting with just one satisfied customer and progressing *ad infinitum*.

So what goes wrong? They're too proud to ask? They're too shy to ask? They failed to satisfy the customer, or they simply forgot to ask? The latter is the most likely explanation. There is still a lot of sentiment in business. Many customers would be only too pleased to pass on information helpful to the salesman keen enough to ask for it. These novel incentive schemes are designed to remind your salesmen to ask for recommendations from existing customers. They can be used many times to prod and encourage your sales people into action.

Suggested campaign titles

'The Great Night Out'/'Bunny Club Bonanza'/'Rabbit Rabbit Rabbit'

Prize

A night out at the Playboy Club in London, for the winning salesman and his best customer, including dinner and overnight accommodation at a top class hotel in Central London. The Playboy Club needs no introduction. The salesman and his customer can relax and enjoy the sophisticated charms of London's night life. A memorable evening of mutual enjoyment establishes even closer bonds between salesman and customer.

The customer can join in the fun of this novel competition. A recommendation form is provided and signed by the customer when passing on a lead. The salesman obtaining most leads in this way during the campaign period wins the prize (leads subject to sales management audit).

Requirements

The cost of a night out for two at the Playboy Club (including spending money, dinner, overnight accommodation at a top class hotel). Promotion material to launch the incentive scheme to your sales staff. Playboy Club 'keys' sent to salesmen as a reminder during the campaign. Forms for completion by customers when passing on a sales lead. Newsletters overprinted with your company name carrying details of progress during the campaign and distributed to participants.

Cost category ££

(b)

Suggested campaign titles

'Be a Sport'/'Sporting Club'/'King of Sport'

'If a man does not make new acquaintances through life, he will soon find himself alone. A man, sir, should keep his friendship in constant repair'

(Samuel Johnson)

Probably the most pleasant way of meeting new prospective customers is through friendly referrals from regular customers. It's only fair to let them have an opportunity to enjoy a special reward.

Prize

A fabulous sporting day out for the winning salesman and his customer. Visiting a famous sporting event such as a cup final, open golf championship, test cricket, rugby international, tennis championships, motor racing. Includes best seats at the event, chauffeur driven transport, five course lunch with champagne, VIP treatment to make it a real day out to remember.

Requirements

Complete cost of a day out for two at a major sporting event (refer to directory in this book for incentive companies offering sporting 'package'). Attractive, colourful, promotional material for campaign launch. Novelty gifts for distribution during the campaign. News bulletins announcing progress of the campaign and providing newsworthy information. Forms for completion by customers when passing on a sales lead.

Cost category £

(c)

Because the salesman is so dependent on referrals from customers it's a good idea to let the customers share in the prize. This next incentive scheme has been used frequently in the motor industry, but would be a popular idea in any type of business.

Suggested campaign titles

'Go by Rolls'/'A drive to RRemember'/'Drive a Dream'

Prize

A superb Rolls Royce limousine hired for a day, for the winning salesman, customer and wives, to drive and enjoy. Included in the prize would be a visit to a fashionable restaurant.

Requirements

Hire of Rolls Royce. Gourmet dinner for four. Catalogues obtained from a Rolls Royce dealer illustrating the superb qualities of this famous marque. 'RR' motifs printed on sales incentive literature (for private use only). Photographs of the winning salesman and his customer at the wheel. (Professional photographs.)

Cost category ££

6) Stimulate New Sales Ideas

The future of the company and its employees depends on the ability to continue selling products or services.

Employees can contribute useful ideas and suggestions which can help to make the sales department more efficient and more effective. If they can be persuaded really to put their minds to thinking sales, the benefits are twofold. Firstly, some surprisingly good ideas can result. Secondly, a more informed and sympathetic relationship between employees and the sales force will help to avoid the 'them and us' situations which sometimes damage internal relationships and sabotage good service to the customer.

Throw away the dusty old suggestion box and catch the imagination of employees with a sales 'think tank'. This competition gives everyone the opportunity to contribute towards the company's marketing activity. Here's the chance they've all been waiting for to show the sales department how the job should really be done!

The best ideas deserve generous awards, but it's important also to recognise the value of even the smallest contribution. The following are examples of subjects suggested as 'think tank' thought starters. The next step is to publicise the 'think tank' sales competition and encourage as many suggestions as possible:

1 Advertising	6 Sales promotion	11 Display
2 Packaging design	7 Sales office procedure	12 Public relations
3 Product design	8 Communications	13 Cost cutting
4 Distribution	9 Market research	14 New markets
5 Publicity	10 Training	15 Staff incentives

(These subjects would be explained in more detail, with examples, for the benefit of employees.)

Suggested campaign titles

'Sales Think Tank'/'Think Sales'/'Sales Ideas'

Prize

Gift vouchers or prize points awards to enable the winners to select a wide range of goods of their own choice from an attractive gift catalogue. This is a very popular form of incentive prize, particularly for 'non-sales' people who can be more easily motivated by the novelty of such an incentive.

Requirements

A recommended prize point or gift voucher award scheme. (Values to be decided by management.) Publicity material, posters and leaflets to promote and publicise the scheme for four weeks in advance of the commencement. The aim is to arouse and build up interest of employees with a weekly issue of publicity material. Posters, leaflets, and letters, announcing the details of the competition and the prize awards for the winners. Weekly news posters overprinted with the company· name and giving details of number of entries in the competition. Attractive and amusing badges to be issued to participants showing a cartoon character in various moods, e.g. 'Shut up, I'm thinking', 'I'm smart', 'I've had an idea'. A committee (including a 'non-sales' member) should be formed for the purpose of scrutinising and judging all the entries and making the awards at the end of the campaign.

Cost category £±

7) Test Product Knowledge

'For knowledge itself is power'

(Francis Bacon)

The image of the star salesman – achieving magical success, using experience and cunning. Brilliant and forceful, thick skinned and confident, sell anything. The image still lingers today. However, modern technology and more sophisticated buying methods now often require salesmen to be highly qualified technically and possess rather different qualities from the 'sales type' of the good old days (?). Products are generally much more complicated. Without a thorough knowledge of his own and his competitors' products, the salesman is likely to lose orders to a more knowledgeable rival. Knowledge builds confidence. Every ACE salesman has confidence.

Ability. Confidence. Enthusiasm. Perhaps the qualities haven't changed so much over the years. But real confidence, through knowledge and training in all the products or services he sells, is necessary to become an ACE salesman.

Training takes time, and you can't afford to take up too much available selling time by arranging sales courses for people. The individual must accept some responsibility for self teaching. Studying new product details can become an onerous task for the salesman keen to get face to face with as many customers as possible. It's always necessary, but often neglected by even the most self disciplined salesman. So how do we prevent this neglect? It could result in lost sales before the sales manager discovers the root of the problem. But should you really reward them for doing something which is part of the discipline of their job? The answer is yes, if they're prepared to do it *better* than they've ever done before. That's what this incentive is all about. That's what the ideas in this book are all about – achieving a *better* sales performance.

Suggested campaign titles

'Be an ACE Salesman'/'Did you know?'/'Know your Products'

Objective

A salesman doesn't have to win the 'Brain of Britain' quiz to win prizes in this competition. He simply has to answer a number of questions about products or services (yours or your competitors'). The advantage of this simple quiz game is that it can be conducted at a meeting, by 'phone in' or by mail. The objective is to improve the product knowledge of the salesman, which improves confidence, and results in improved sales.

Prize

A bottle of champagne with a special label printed in the company name and inscribed with the name of the winning salesman. A quiz each week, during the campaign period keeps the fun alive and ensures that salesmen maintain the standards required.

Requirements

Three bottles of champagne with the specially designed labels. An attractive leaflet giving details of the incentive and announcing the contest. Preparation of questions for product knowledge quiz. Questionnaire forms overprinted with the company name, for use in each product knowledge quiz. A newsletter after each quiz, listing the competition results, giving names in order of merit.

Cost category £

8) Increase New Business Prospecting

'When the going gets tough, the tough get going.'

They prospect hard for new business.

They don't lose enthusiasm.

They don't take no for an answer.

They don't believe the market is saturated.

They don't think competitors have an advantage.

They don't believe times are bad.

They don't finish early on Fridays.

They don't call on customers without being properly prepared.

They don't complain about their 'bad' territory.

They don't wait for inspiration.

They don't envy other salesmen.

They don't adopt a cynical attitude.

They don't only call on regular customers.

That's what the tough don't do

Do your salesmen work hard at new business prospecting? Do you do enough to encourage them? Finding and selling to new customers is a tough job. Accomplishments in this vital part of selling are worthy of additional rewards.

This stimulating and rewarding incentive scheme can be switched full on and interest sustained throughout the period of the campaign. Salesmen who may have previously been reluctant to canvass for new business suddenly want to show their mettle. Others step up their work rate by phenomenal amounts as they strive on the trail of new business prospects. Targets can either be based on new orders received, or number of new contacts established during the campaign period. Either way it's a certainty that the company will benefit from a vigorous sales push for new business.

Suggested campaign titles

'Prospect for Gold'/'Bonanza'/'Operation Gold Rush'

Prize

Shares in a goldmine. The same reasons given previously make this a cracking good prize, ideally suitable for a new business incentive scheme. It has an immediate, dramatic effect on the salesmen's attitude towards new business prospecting.

Requirements

Shares in a goldmine purchased in the name of the winning salesman. The shares will be acquired on the recommendation of a professional stockbroker at the end of the contest. Illustrated folders printed with your name, giving details about the incentive campaign for distribution to your salesmen. Weekly news bulletins to carry the campaign message. A humorous illustrated poster 'hidden treasure', urging your salesmen to keep prospecting. Low cost gifts sent to salesmen during the campaign and reminding them and their families that the contest for prospects is on (e.g. gold charm, gold pen, perfume with gold cap).

Cost category ££

9) New Product Launch

New land – lots of time + money

(a)

'10–9–8–7–6–5–4–3–2–1–Zero We have lift off.

Make sure you have 'lift off' with your next new product launch. The chances of a new product being successful are improved if a good sales incentive scheme is included in the promotional programme. The high failure rate of new products is proof enough of the need for a thorough sales preparation and efficient launch plan. Salesmen are busy enough handling existing products or services and don't have the time to push a new line without detriment to regular sales ... Or are they? The answer could be to offer an incentive which encourages them to work harder or plan their time more efficiently. An incentive can provide extra impetus to a new product launch and reduce the risk of failure.

This simple, easy to operate incentive, satisfies all the major requirements of a successful sales incentive campaign. It aims to maintain the level of sales of existing products or services and give 'lift off' to the new product or service. Targets for the new product are set in line with market forecast. Salesmen can only qualify if they achieve their targets and maintain previous sales levels on existing products. Everyone has a fair chance of winning something. Interest is maintained throughout the period of the campaign. Rewards are directly related to achievements.

The incentive prizes can be arranged through one of the national fashion chain shops with branches in all major towns.

'A competing salesman is a better salesman.'

Suggested campaign titles

'What's New'/'New Opportunity'/'Lift Off'

Prize

A new suit. A new topcoat. New suede coat. New leather jacket. New sports clothes, holiday clothes, casual clothes.

New clothes of all descriptions to provide everything your winning salesman needs for his wardrobe. New clothes for the smartest salesman.

The promotion takes full advantage of attractive advertising material offering the fashion and flair to help the sales effort achieve real sales productivity for the new product launch.

Requirements

'Tailor made' gift vouchers for new clothes according to client requirements. Illustrated folders printed with your company name, giving details about the incentive campaign for distribution to your salesmen. Weekly news bulletins to carry the campaign message and announce up to date results and progress. Interesting and attractive 'reminder' gifts mailed direct to your salesmen during the campaign period. These would be in the form of low cost clothing accessories e.g. handkerchief, tie, socks. These mailing packages would give added interest and impact to the incentive campaign. An attractive poster publicising results of the competition. Humorous 'Impakt' type attention getters from company management to the sales force. An attractive display of men's fashion clothing and a men's fashion presentation at your new product launch meeting.

Cost category £±

(b)

'I see you stand like greyhounds in the slips'
(William Shakespeare)

Interesting, useful, attractive, stimulating motivators for salesmen. Simple, effective, flexible, sales performance bonds which can be used by management to put real impetus behind a new product launch. It's fair because every salesman wins something. The best salesman wins the most. The contest ends when the initial overall target is reached. You can control your budget from the launch date by setting the total sales target and selecting the total prize value in advance. Will this incentive help to encourage your salesmen to increase their sales effort?

'Most people exert only 15% of their combined intelligence, skills and aptitudes in their employment'
(William James)

Suggested campaign titles

'Rocket Launch'/'Springboard'/'Flying Start'

Prize

Exciting new incentive bonds (Bonus Bonds) with cash values to suit a sales contest and a budget. Available in many different schemes and can be used separately or combined to form an attractive award. Economical to use, strong motivators, offering wide scope and choice to your sales force.

Requirements

A variety of incentive bonds to suit your budget and your choice. Production of colourful launch material to present the incentive campaign professionally and ensure real impact behind your new product launch. Follow up news bulletins designed to sustain interest and enthusiasm throughout the period of the incentive campaign.

Cost category £±

10) Improve Customer Relations

What does your junior clerk in the office know about customer relations? What should your junior clerk know? What does your junior clerk care? Answer, 'not much' to any of these questions, then ask yourself if it's possible to improve your customer relations by making everyone aware of the importance of good customer service in all its forms.

Many of your employees may not have direct contact with your customers, but that doesn't mean they have no influence on customer relations. If more people in the company are encouraged to regard the customer as a VIP, then you are on the right track to improving customer relations. Recently, a major company in the electrical industry launched a campaign called 'Get it right'. It aimed to reduce the number of minor mistakes in the processing of customer orders, such as errors in quoting stock numbers, typing errors, checking errors, computer input errors. All the irritating little mistakes that are possible in the order process chain. Error factor reduced = Customer relations improved.

This is just one example of how everyone in the company can influence customer relations through a more responsible, more conscious, more caring attitude to customer service. The following incentive is a light hearted idea, simple, effective, and fun for your staff and your customers.

Suggested campaign titles

'What's in it for you?'/'Service with a smile'/'Secret Service'

Prize

A 'lucky numbers' prize of a holiday weekend (for two) in Paris for the winning member of your staff, your customer, and the salesman who took the order. Every customer order taken during the campaign is numbered and included in a draw which takes place at the conclusion of the campaign. Each member of your staff is 'attached' to a customer or block of customers. A draw takes place to determine the winning customer. Another draw takes place to select the winning staff member. The salesman who took the order wins the sales prize. The customers don't have to do anything to compete (except place orders). Employees don't have to compete, but they are encouraged to become more aware of the need to look after customers' interests.

Requirements

A weekend package tour holiday in Paris arranged through a leading travel agent (i.e. three Paris weekends for two). Incentive promotion pre-launch material includes poster, letters to customers and sales information bulletins. Production of colourful and amusing launch material and follow-up material to ensure a professional presentation and operation of the campaign.

Cost category £

11) Promote Special Products or Services

'Great things are done when men and mountains meet'
(William Blake)

Man has always found extra effort when matching himself with the efforts of others. It's doubtful if the four minute mile would ever have been achieved without the spur of competition. Salesmen are no exception to this rule. It's been proved many times that a well run sales contest brings out extra effort from salesmen, which can show a handsome return on the investment. A sales incentive campaign can be the ideal way of pushing a selected product or service, and have an immediate and dramatic effect on sales. It may be used as a tool to focus attention on a neglected item, or add impetus to a special offer deal, or encourage the clearance of old stock.

Suggested campaign titles

'Bingo Special'/'The Great Bingo Contest'/'Bingo Winners'

The salesman and his customers can both participate in the 'Bingo' sales competition. Customers are issued with a set of bingo cards at commencement. The cards are pre-printed with details of product numbers, quantities, etc. Points are awarded for each completed line or combination of lines. The competition closes when a customer succeeds in completing his card with a 'full house'. The salesman also scores points geared to the customer's success.

This incentive is very simple to administer. Everyone has a fair chance of winning something. It's also good for customer relations.

Prize

Gift vouchers or prize points awards to enable the winners to choose goods from an attractive gift catalogue.

Requirements

Gift vouchers or prize point certificates redeemed through a merchandise/award company. All the necessary promotional material to enable the client to launch and administer the scheme can be provided by the supplier.

Cost category ££

12) Boost Salesmen's Morale

'They conquer who believe they can'   (Emerson)

The power of positive thinking has been recognised for centuries. It's surprising that even now, in the space age, we often fail to appreciate the power of the mind. In the beginning, somebody thought to himself, 'I will sail round the world.' Others have focused their thought power on similar historic achievements: 'I will reach the Pole', 'I will climb Mount Everest', 'run a four minute mile', 'go to the moon', 'swim the Channel'. How much proof do we want before we are convinced that a positive mind and a determined approach to the job will bring success? Higher authorities have recognised man's mind power.

'If ye have faith, nothing shall be impossible unto you.'
(The Bible)

'I think victory, I get victory.'   (Jefferson)

'Throw your mind over the bar and your heart will follow.'   (Peale)

To be successful, a salesman has to possess exceptional qualities: enthusiasm, self discipline, ability, confidence, determination, tenacity, will power, optimism, initiative, physical and mental strength. But he's only human! Sometimes even the best salesman's spirit sags. He loses an important order. He feels a bit low. He's unbalanced by a domestic crisis. So what does he need to sustain him when morale droops? The power to shrug off problems. The power to keep on selling. The power of confidence. The power of the mind. The proven power of positive thinking. Most salesmen know about positive thinking and understand the importance of it. But that doesn't mean they don't need moral support to support their morale! Maintaining salemen's morale can be one of the most difficult of management tasks, also the most important.

The following low cost idea has succeeded countless times and will always be recommended as a morale booster and sales motivator *par excellence*.

Suggested campaign titles

'Think Positive'/'Believe in Success'/'Aim for the Top'

This is an incentive event, not a contest. A very special one day sales conference at a luxury hotel is announced about a month in advance. Salesmen are informed that invitation will be on the basis of individual performance and suitability (delegates' names proposed by the sales manager). In practice, *all* the salesmen will be invited.

The event will be professionally organised by a leading specialist in the field of sales training. It will be promoted in such a way as to make salesmen feel privileged to attend. A guest celebrity will be invited to speak. The training session will be dynamic, morale boosting and educational. The aim is to ignite salesmen's performance and inspire successful thinking.

Prize

Attendance at an exclusive one day training conference in a luxury hotel.

Requirements

A one day sales conference tailor made to requirements, presented by leading sales trainers, specialising in the field of positive thinking, positive attitudes, creative selling and salesman motivation. Guest speaker. Pre-conference publicity material, designed in attractive folders, over-printed with your company name. Post-conference follow up material, to maintain salesmen's interest and continue the development of top producers.

Cost category ££

Checklist

Every incentive scheme should be carefully planned in advance. A good approach is to work to a checklist something like the following:

- *What is the objective?* e.g. increase sales, increase call rate, launch a new product.
- *What is the campaign title?* 'Prospecting Pays', 'Join the Gold Rush', 'World Cup Awards', 'Sales Drive', etc.
- *Description of the incentive scheme* (or competition description).
- *Targets* (or what the salesmen have to do to win awards).
- *Cost of the incentive* (best to enlist help from the management accountant).
- *Potential extra profit* from the incentive (if appropriate).
- *Starting date and closing date.* (Depends very much on objectives. Try to avoid an incentive over too long a period which may cause interest to wane. Don't keep it so short that it fails to be effective.)
- *Who is going to run it?* A fair amount of administration work will usually be involved. It may be a good idea for the sales manager to form an operating committee which includes 'non-sales' managers.
- *What type of incentive scheme to use?*
  a) Individual prize scheme, with maybe first, second and third prizes. The weakness of this type of scheme is that it usually only motivates the top few salesmen and often demotivates the rest. It may also be regarded as unfair by salesmen who will argue that their territory/allocation/local market conditions/advertising support, are not as favourable as those of other salesmen.
  b) Prize points schemes: salesmen simply compete against their own individual targets. They win points immediately they beat target, which can be exchanged for goods or hoarded towards the acquisition of a big prize. Everybody can win

something. Interest is maintained at a high level throughout the period of the contest. The competition is focused on personal performance. This avoids any possible resentment caused by one salesman pushing a colleague out of the race for prizes. It's a type of competition which is easy to promote. A disadvantage can be loss of competitive spirit between contestants.

c) Team prize scheme: this can be arranged to reward the whole team collectively for a team achievement. Alternatively, the sales force can be split into two teams to compete against each other. This type of contest encourages team spirit. Also, the salesmen are likely to push any poor performers themselves. A problem can arise, however, if the star salesmen resents 'carrying' the rest of the team.

● *What is the prize?*
Make sure all the salesmen are interested in the prize. If it is in the form of merchandise, offer alternatives. A holiday could offer a choice of venues. Don't offer cash as an alternative, the joy of winning fades too soon. Also, cash is more likely to create tax problems.

● *What are the campaign rules?*
Be clear and specific. It's preferable to avoid any future disputes caused by misinterpretation or ambiguity in promotional literature.

● *Launch of the incentive campaign*
To be done with as much style and flair as the budget will allow.

● *Presentation of awards*
To be done with as much style and flair as the budget will allow.

● *Promoting the campaign*
To be done with as much style and flair as the budget will allow, *and as often as possible.*

● *Communications*
Write about it, talk about it, clearly. Let salesmen know regularly, how they are doing.

Some case histories

Here are descriptions and comments from three sales managers, a car maker, an electronics industrialist, and a cosmetics producer. The writers have produced their own factual reports, each recording details of a successful sales incentive campaign which has been organised and implemented in their company. They illustrate sales incentives at work in consumer selling, industrial selling and direct selling situations.

First, let's hear from Ken Malia, Sales Operations Manager in the UK for the Vauxhall–Opel division of General Motors Ltd.

Vauxhall–Opel passenger car marketing dealer incentive campaign

'When a manufacturer is selling his products through a franchised network, motivation becomes difficult. There are three main paths which can be followed once it has been decided that increased sales are the objective. Incentives can be offered to the franchise holder or dealer to be used by him for customer benefits or motivation of his staff, or even to retain as additional profits.

Alternatively, incentives can be given by the manufacturer direct to dealer staff over and above his normal commissions. The third method is to offer benefits direct to the customer, heavily advertise this and provide 'warm' prospects for the dealer.

Each of these has its advantages and drawbacks and many variations on the three approaches have been tried.

Perhaps the variation most commonly used in the motor trade, and one that generally gets results, is the variation I will describe here.

I refer to holiday awards – or more particularly what might be considered exotic holiday awards. These are usually supported by prize points given against vehicles sold. I suppose everybody likes an unexpected holiday, especially one that takes care of the participant from door to door with every luxury thrown in.

The latest of this type of incentive offered by Vauxhall Motors Limited was called 'Lifestyle Challenge'. This took place during the first quarter of 1980 and was planned deliberately, as Vauxhall Motors had been short of product in the record motor industry sales year of 1979. In common with other manufacturers, supplies were catching up, and soon passing demand which was by then on the decline. Obviously, competitive activity was expected to increase rapidly and we were not disappointed in that respect.

The thing about this type of incentive is that everybody should feel they are in with a chance to win and the prize should be worth winning. Inevitably, the former is the more difficult to achieve. So, even for those who feel they will not win the big prizes, there must still be incentive to participate. Another problem is to judge the right length of time for the campaign. Make it too short and little is achieved, too long and participants tend to relax. Always, it is important to include a Fast Start Award. Then ensure the remaining timespan is just right to maintain enthusiasm and what is more important, effort.

Bearing all of this in mind, it is necessary to devise a campaign which will produce increased sales over the period. Obviously, there is little point in running just to stand still, and increased sales help to defray the cost.

Whenever Vauxhall Motors decide on this action, we turn to the professionals. We brief several companies whose business it is to handle this type of operation, and we select the best presentation on the day. Naturally, we decide dealers' targets and groupings and maintain full operational control.

Once the plan has been agreed, probably after several meetings between Vauxhall and the Incentive Company, we swing into action.

The first step is to determine each dealer's target for the period. This is decided by Vauxhall after considering several factors, including current performance, future potential and Vauxhall needs in his area. So that all dealers, who vary greatly in volume, can compete with each other on a fair and equitable basis, we break them down by groups. This leaves large dealers competing with other large dealers and so on. In the case of 'Lifestyle Challenge', the dealer force of around six hundred was divided into seven groups. Not all groups have the same number of dealers. Usually there are fewer dealers in the higher volume groups and more in the lower volume groups.

We can then give the Incentive Company the basis for the next step, which is to set up the administration so that results can be monitored on a regular basis. This monitoring of results and regular reporting back to the dealers is of prime importance. Each group has only so many winners and for those striving to be amongst these, they need to know their position regularly. So weekly bulletins based on dealer sales to date, and always headed with the 'Lifestyle Challenge' logo, were issued.

In addition to this, regular colourful teasers were mailed to all dealers along with appropriately designed specific holiday brochures. All of this was designed to maintain the atmosphere and encourage all dealers to carry on the sales momentum. Dealer sales recorders were despatched to all dealers to assist them with their own records.

Having set the scene so to speak, it is vital to announce the plan in detail, and with the right atmosphere, to all dealers. The beginning of every year usually creates a need for conveying to dealers the start of that year's marketing plans. 1980 was no excepton and several dealer meetings were held throughout the country, which were addressed by one of two teams of Vauxhall executives. The high spot of these presentations was an audio/visual description of the chosen Holiday and Prize Points Awards. This was followed by details of how to enter and win 'Lifestyle Challenge'.

'Lifestyle Challenge'

In addition to the audio/visual description of the chosen holiday and Prize Point awards, dealers were given a brightly-coloured, informative pack of literature, together with a personalised envelope containing details of their group and targets, before leaving the meeting. The audio/visual presentation won their interest and was backed up with the hard facts for them to digest.

As I have already mentioned, the programme ran from 1 January through to 31 March and it set the pace for the remainder of the year.

An easily attainable 'Fast Start Target' was given to get the dealers motivated and in the 'swing' of things. In addition, a 'Campaign Target' was given. This was more realistic and something for the dealer to work towards.

For every eligible car registered within the campaign period, the dealership earned Prize Points – the number of points relating directly to the level of target achievement. A set number of Prize Points were awarded for every unit up to the 'Fast Start Target'; and this number increased considerably from the 'Fast Start Target' to the 'Campaign Target'. On achieving the 'Campaign Target', all Prize Point values were automatically doubled, retrospectively from the 'Fast Start Target', and were awarded for every sale over the above the 'Campaign Target'. At the end of the programme those dealerships that achieved the highest percentage of sales over 'Campaign Target' were given the special holiday awards.

Because the number of dealers within each league varied so much, in some of the leagues we had more than one top dealership award, whilst in others only the one was available. This, of course, also applied to the numbers of runner-up dealership awards.

For the top dealership awards, the chief executive was flown, on Concorde, to a holiday in Rio de Janeiro, together with a partner; whilst the sales manager, together with partner, was given a holiday in Monte Carlo. The top salesman/woman, again with partner, was also awarded a holiday in Monte Carlo but for a shorter period of time.

In addition to the holiday awards the dealership was given a bonus award of Prize Points to be divided by the sales team at the discretion of the dealer principal.

For each runner-up dealership, the chief executive and his partner were taken to Canada for a holiday, whilst the sales manager and top salesman or women were taken to Monte Carlo, again with their partners.

The total administration set-up was handled by the Incentive Company although, naturally, we provided the raw figures of dealers' sales performance progress on a weekly basis.

For the recording of Prize Point allocations to any one dealer, the Incentive Company devised a system similar to that used for banking. We had a 'Lifestyle Challenge' Prize Point Award Bank, whereby each individual dealer had his own account debited or credited accordingly. To keep dealers informed of their 'spending', regular 'statements of accounts' were sent. In addition,the Incentive Company mailed the weekly League Standing Reports to inform dealers of their continued progress within their own leagues.

The incentive proved to be a success in 1980 as our market ratio indicated in the months during the campaign. In the period following the incentive, our market ratio fell, and the actual volume dropped by nearly half, thus proving that the incentive certainly motivated our dealer sales force for the campaign months.'

Now Philip Bullus, Managing Director (Sales), Bourns Electronics Ltd., reports on incentives in the electronics industry.

Marketing incentives in the electronics industry

'Whether sales of silicon chips are up or down, marketing incentives can motivate sales personnel to increase their efforts. In the highly competitive and sophisticated electronics industry new products are constantly being introduced. Companies who fall behind in the technology race cannot expect to stay in business for long. To stay ahead, the leaders must invest heavily in research and development, not only to design and develop new products, but also to seek new materials, manufacturing processes and fast methods, keeping a close eye on their competitors and close liaison with the users. Marketing has never been so important. Incentives can be used as a means to increase product knowledge, market penetration and profit and help to motivate staff long after any awards have been won.

Successfully to sell electronic products, it is generally necessary to use qualified electronics engineers with some design experience. New products first need to be introduced to customers' design departments. It can often take two years or more before the purchasing department begins to issue worthwhile orders. Military or telecommunications projects may take much longer. An incentive scheme based simply on sales volume could be detrimental to a company's long term interests if it resulted in the sales effort being applied to established products at the expense of new products.

Distributors account for approximately 25 per cent of sales of electronic components in the UK and are likely to increase further. Although biased towards standard products for which a market has already been established, their sales personnel still need a technical background. The larger distributors employ product specialists to support the sales force, liaise with their franchises and answer customers' queries. The present total annual 'running cost' of a sales engineer is around £20,000. Prices of petrol, telephone calls, food and accommodation are unlikely to diminish and with a shortage of qualified engineers, salaries and benefits are certain to increase. It is therefore imperative that as marketing costs rise, more steps are taken to direct and motivate the field sales force, keeping it as up to date as the products it sells and attuned to changes in company objectives and marketing strategy. Incentives are not essential to achieve this, but they do help. The scattergun principle has been applied in the past, with some manufacturers producing new products then finding an insufficient demand or, just as bad, losing to competitors with smaller, better performance, lower cost designs.

Electronics engineers had a tendency to sell by intuition, often being free to operate without supervision in a geographical area. Marketing techniques are being applied along with a more disciplined approach. A period of recession can be good for an industry accustomed to a high growth rate. Customers demand more attention and a better service and are more likely to obtain what they need than feel obliged to accept what they are given. Again, incentive programmes can be used to ensure that sales personnel find out what customers want and help to focus their employer's resources in the best way.

Sophisticated products do not need sophisticated incentives. Electronics is a young, good humoured industry receptive to new products and ideas. The average age of sales personnel is below thirty-five.

The semiconductor industry still shows signs of immaturity, but members are now less inclined towards indiscriminate incentives. These became self-defeating when the most effective sales engineers were sent to some exotic isle to enjoy an unexpected extra holiday at the company's expense. Two or three years ago, distributors' sales engineers and inside sales staff were bombarded with all kinds of incentives as their franchises vied with each other for their attention. Many such schemes had little effect on sales and performance measurements were often not agreed beforehand. The suprised recipient of a digital watch was pleased at first. He continued receiving them however and began to treat the company with scorn and frustration as they declined to give him cash in lieu and declared him to be ungrateful. (Prior to reaching this low point, the multiple winner demonstrated with four watches on each arm.)

Incentive programmes have evolved to the point where the major distributors decline to allow their sales force to participate in anything but those of their own creation. (It is unlikely that the winner will again have to hurry back from one free holiday so that he can immediately go on another!)

As in any other industry, almost anyone can dream up an incentive campaign and hundreds of companies are ready to offer premiums, competition prizes and motivators. The hard part is making it work.

My own company introduced an incentive campaign to increase sales of semiconductor products. We needed to improve the product knowledge of the sales force and to increase the face-to-face selling effort. Simple targets were established based on the number of personal customer contacts made (the most effective way to sell state-of-the-art products). On a score chart, points were awarded for quotations, quote follow-up orders, etc., with additional bonus points for new ideas, individual effort, success stories, results of quiz contests, etc. The programme ran for a period of eight weeks with weekly bulletins, score sheets, a 'league table' and minor prizes aimed at retaining the interest of every participant, not merely those near the top of the table. Clothing vouchers were presented at the end of the campaign which made this a relatively low cost incentive.

Sales engineers' wives (valuable assets) were encouraged to help. Inside staff were briefed from the start and became intensely involved. By the end of the eight-week period, the whole company had become more sales minded, and customers were impressed with the speed of responses and the enthusiasm shown.

To suit our particular requirements, points were awarded as follows:

(a) Customer contacts: one point awarded for each face-to-face discussion about the products with a customer. (Subject to checks by the sales supervisors. It did not become necessary to deduct points for false claims.)

(b) Quotations: one point for each written or telex quotation.

(c) Quote follow-ups: two points for each completed follow-up copy returned to the office within fourteen days of the date of issue.

(d) Seminars/customer site exhibitions: five points for each customer seminar or site exhibition arranged and confirmed during the period of the contest.

(e) Telephone orders: two points for each order telephoned to the office by the sales engineer.

(f) Joint visits: one additional point for each customer visit made with a product specialist.

(g) Bonus points: five bonus points per week depending on product quiz results, success stories, special action, etc.

Form filling was necessary, but kept to a minimum. Everyone entered into the spirit of the campaign and found it enjoyable. Sales did not increase dramatically, but this was not expected. The customer base increased, several new ideas were adopted, the sales call rate increased and sales engineers' product knowledge improved. Since that time sales have consistently met targets and the products are used by every major equipment manufacturer in the industry. All the original objectives were achieved.

A similar incentive campaign is shortly to be launched for a long established but often neglected product line. Product knowledge is again high on the list of priorities. This time tape recordings will be used and sales engineers will be encouraged to listen during driving time. Points will be awarded for correct answers to questions 'hidden' on the tapes. The programme will be integrated with advertising and direct mail. Major competitors will be subjected to a determined attack which will surprise them. Weekly incentive awards will be sent to sales engineers and distributors during an eight-week programme. For example, car accessories are easily related to an intensive hunt for business: a compass, an inspection lamp, driving gloves, a tyre gauge. Wives will be roped in via Interflora (to signify growth and the sweet smell of success), and for individual success during the campaign, personalised gifts will be awarded. Final awards will be made by the Company President at the Annual Sales Conference.

Some imagination and creativity are needed to help deliver the messages. This is a necessary element of any marketing function and should not require the services of expensive independent consultants except for special reasons.

Every participant will be a winner and the campaign will be stimulating and enjoyable. Product knowledge and customer contact will increase. High quality products do not sell themselves, but with an excellent product base, competitively priced, a properly motivated sales force is the best asset any company can have, particularly where the technical content of the product is high. Market share can only be increased at the expense of competitors. An incentive programme is the best and most cost-effective way to obtain a bigger bite of the market.

Along with a host of others, my company was invited to a recession. The invitation was declined. Incentives are used to keep morale high and take advantage of the many opportunities available. A two-way information exchange is essential. The combined efforts of a sales team headed in the right direction is the surest path to success in the electronics or any other industry.'

Cosmetics company – a typical incentive campaign

This particular cosmetics business relies heavily on a very professional direct sales operation. The following incentive is typical of the effort required to motivate sales in this tough, highly competitive market. For reasons of confidentiality, names have been withheld. However, the sales incentive programme reproduced here provides a good insight into the workings of a recent sales incentive campaign. It has been their practice to organise three major campaigns every year.

'Spring Fair Promotion'

The incentive was introduced to the sales force (mostly part time saleswomen) during a sales conference at a top class hotel. All the style and flair that go into a good theatrical production helped the incentive campaign to start with a whirl. A thoroughly professional approach, polished by hours of rehearsal and planning, generated an electric enthusiasm amongst the audience. The conference room was packed with all manner of prize 'goodies' waiting to be won, and ranging from the practical to the exotic.

Attractively printed brochures, lively music, uniformed executives, colourful banners and posters, were all designed to reflect the 'Spring Fair' theme. The promotion was repeated in several areas to cover a national sales force in excess of 1,500 part time 'beauty consultants'.

Planned to cover a twelve week period, the campaign message was hammered out repeatedly each week to every member of the sales team.

Programme

Week 1   'Spring Fair' launch.
                    Introduction and presentation at a luxury hotel. First sales targets allocated.

Week 2	'Early Spring' results announced.
Week 3	First 'Spring Fair' individual prize achievements published. Area Team selection takes place. Team sales targets allocated.
Week 4	Sales bulletin carries details of team activities.
Weeks 5–7	Regular weekly bulletins showing team results. Also listing individual sales performance on leader board.
Week 8	Winning area team over first two months announced.
Weeks 9–11	Weekly bulletins listing national team competition results.
Week 12	Telegrams to all members of sales team with details of special offer during final week.
Week 13	Presentation of prize awards during sales conference at luxury hotal.

The incentive campaign had three clear objectives:

1 Increase total sales by 20 per cent over previous twelve weeks' sales.
2 Promote sales of a new product and quickly establish it within the product range.
3 Recruit 200 suitable new members to the sales team.

The first individual sales targets required a 10 per cent improvement in the first two weeks, measured against their own performance in the previous two weeks. They then progressed to Stage 2 which was membership of an area team. However, membership could still be achieved, if they recruited another person or achieved a high level of sales of the new product. Area supervisors were urged to 'pull through' at least 90 per cent of the saleswomen to the area team competition.

Area teams were then allocated new sales targets and put to work competing enthusiastically in the next round of the incentive campaign. Again, it was possible to make up points by recruiting or raising performance on the new product.

Stage 3 was selection of Area Teams to go forward into a national competition. In addition, a special individual prize was announced, open to any saleswoman who had succeeded in coming best in her team, regardless of whether the team became eligible for further honours.

The campaign was organised and promoted in such a way as to keep hopes alive for every member of the sales team, until the final week of the contest. The vitally important objectives were impressed upon managers and supervisors. (Their relaxed manner and fun loving style concealed the pressures of the operation!)

Final week of the 'Spring Fair', and frenzied sales activity resulted, as teams and individuals vied with each other to win the top prizes. Results were announced at another razzle dazzle conference. Female hearts pounded as if they were all in the finals of the 'Miss World' contest, breathlessly hanging on the announcement of results, in reverse order of course!

A holiday in Bermuda, a luxury kitchen, video tape recorder, microwave oven, water bed, solarium and lounge suite were offered and seized with delight by the joyful recipients. Expensive 'spot prizes' were given to help assuage the feelings of disappointed losers. Try again next time, 'Summer Winners' campaign is starting soon!

Note: the efficiency of the sales administration system in a contest such as this is of crucial importance. Results have to be monitored accurately, at speed. The sales administration manager has to be prepared to work round the clock if necessary, to meet print and publicity deadlines.

This type of 'mass motivation' incentive campaign works well with part time saleswomen. They enjoy themselves and like to let their hair down after months of hard work. It's doubtful whether the same style of incentive would work for cynical salesmen, but anyone who has been privileged to attend such a 'crusade' of joyful selling will come away with much food for thought.

Part III
Managing Sales Incentives

The place of incentives in the marketing plan

Planned marketing is the process of reviewing past and present market position, setting objectives for the future, and planning how to achieve those objectives. But the plan must be flexible enough to enable managers to respond quickly to changes in the market and it's often in these situations that incentives can be most effective.

A typical marketing plan

A typical marketing plan is likely to contain the following elements:

- *Review*
  A review of past performance, in terms of sales and profit of company products, measured against previous market and potential. Including an analysis of the company's performance measured against competition during previous years.

Also, taking a critical look at the company's strengths and weaknesses: productdevelopment, financial resources, customer image, staffing levels, pricing, distribution, advertising and sales promotion, areas of operation, research and development and production capabilities.

● *Assumptions*
An examination of the industrial environment including economic, technological, social and political forecasts.

● *Overall strategy*
A statement of short and long term aims and objectives and an outline of the plan for achieving them (e.g. product development, financial aims, manpower planning, marketing support).

● *Sales strategy*
Detailed forecast of unit sales objectives and revenue, sales and marketing expenditure, sales force structure and controls.

● *Promotional strategy*
An activity plan to co-ordinate production, sales and cash flow in a logical sequence. The strategy should include a contingency plan to give 'back up' support and quick response to rapid changes in market situation.

How to use incentives in achieving marketing objectives

Attitude

Many managers are reluctant to use incentives. However, most of the arguments against incentives come from managers who have previously been involved in unsuccessful schemes because they have been poorly run, or badly timed. Consequently, they're likely to reject for ever this potentially valuable motivational tool.

*(F) Not
pleased.*

Analysis of failed incentives has revealed some surprisingly bad decisions. For example, one company ran a sales incentive scheme which resulted in lowering of morale, poor sales performance and dissatisfied salesmen. The truth was that the sales targets had been set too low in the first place, then halfway through the contest management felt obliged to raise targets because salesmen were winning too much, too soon. Disillusionment was the inevitable result, and a disgruntled sales force spent the remaining period of the incentive contest grumbling instead of working. The lesson from this experience is simple. Take care to ensure that targets are fair both to the salesmen and the company. Wrecking salesmen's morale by raising targets to cover up management mistakes is perhaps too high a price to pay. The reverse situation can occur, when possibly through no fault of their own, salesmen cannot deliver the additional goods they have sold. Maybe unforeseen production difficulties have delayed supplies, or import quotas have fallen behind plan. In these circumstances, a revised incentive scheme, agreed by the salesmen, could aim at offering rewards for effort. Alternatively, an extension of the time allowed to deliver orders could be arranged. This way, salesmen are likely to be more appreciative and co-operate to overcome the problems.

Managers may also fight shy of incentives because they don't wish to appear extravagant, especially during times when the company is asking for economies. The salesmen may win a holiday in Barbados, Tahiti, Bangkok or some such exotic place. This could be regarded as an irresponsible waste of company money by other employees perhaps already resentful because of cut backs and restrictions in other departments. It's important that management are able to justify such apparent indulgence. They must be able clearly to demonstrate the tangible benefits which have resulted from the operation of an incentive contest. Alternatively, they may have to look for other rewards which can motivate salesmen to greater effort. It's common practice these days to reward the workforce for improved productivity. There's no reason why the sales force shouldn't be rewarded also for improved sales productivity. (A top quality training course at an attractive venue may act as a suitable prize instead of a holiday.) Productivity is king. Today, almost every pay deal is linked to increase in output from harder work or improved efficiency. But linking pay to productivity has the effect of raising on-going costs such as pensions, insurance, and other salary-linked employee benefits. Incentives don't increase future costs. They are temporary. The company can run several incentives during the year and spend money on contests and prizes to produce desired results. But there it ends. No continuing costs result. Neither is there any commitment or contract or 'remuneration package' which obliges the company to repeat the process. The idea behind an incentive scheme is to offer reward for extra effort. Incentive schemes are not a substitute for good management. Incentives can be very useful in certain circumstances. The attitude of the manager is vital to the success or failure of an incentive campaign. If his approach is positive, enthusiastic and well planned, he is. likely to achieve objectives and favour the use of incentives. Any other approach is likely to result in failure and influence his future attitude against incentives.

Sales force objectives

The marketing plan will contain sales force objectives and strategies for achieving them. The plan will rely on salesmen who are remunerated, motivated, trained and managed to achieve individual sales targets for their product or sales area. Some sales efforts are unlikely to be improved by adding an incentive scheme. However, there are occasions when extra effort is needed, perhaps to compensate for a seasonal downturn, clear a stock surplus or combat a competitor's activity. A number of sales incentives can be prepared ready for use at such times. It's often necessary to achieve a quick response in these circumstances, and an imaginative incentive scheme can influence and further motivate a sales force to make extra efforts 'above and beyond the call of duty'. For example, one incentive was aimed at increasing the number of face to face customer contacts. Salesmen were encouraged to stretch their working day by making earlier morning calls and later afternoon calls. The most enthusiastic salesman won a prize for the earliest call on a customer which happened to be 7.30 a.m. Also, for that sales team, it well and truly destroyed the myth that you can't make calls before 9.30 a.m. or after 4.30 p.m.

An incentive cannot be guaranteed to work, therefore it's wise to build in a reserve for costs within the marketing budget. However, in the normal run of events, sales incentive schemes are expected to be paid for from extra sales. Another example of how sales incentives can temporarily influence sales force activity is when a salesman leaves unexpectedly. It may be some time before a replacement can be recruited. In the meantime, other salesmen may have to share responsibilities for a wider sales area. In these circumstances, an incentive can be used as a means of providing extra reward for the extra work, without disturbing the existing remuneration package.

Promotional support

To co-ordinate productivity and sales activity is not an easy task. Get it wrong one way and you could quickly have a warehouse full of unsold goods. Get it wrong the other way, and you're likely to have unsatisfied customers and frustrated salesmen. Planned promotions, controlled production, linked with controlled selling is the aim of every marketing manager. Keeping the balance requires skill, judgement and experience. No one gets it right every time, but the 'fine tune' adjustment which an incentive can add to the sales machine helps to make for smoother running.

The sales promotion activity plan forms an integral part of the marketing plan. It has to be sufficiently flexible to allow rapid response to changing situations. Key promotions are often tied in with advertising, public relations activity, merchandising and incentive schemes. The incentive can be linked to the theme of a customer promotion, perhaps making use of existing sales material artwork, to produce colourful sales incentive literature. When the sales manager feels it's necessary to tread on the sales accelerator, he adds the extra power of an incentive scheme to produce instant response. An alternative situation could occur if for some reason a planned improvement to a regular product cannot be introduced on schedule. It may be necessary to go on promoting the old product. In this case, a special incentive could concentrate salesmen's minds on selling this line linked with a customer promotion to regenerate customer interest. The first stage of a marketing plan is the preparation. The second stage is implementation. Recognising the equal importance of these two factors, the efficient manager will be continually reviewing performance against plan. In the process, he will check on the effectiveness of any incentive schemes. He will have to assess the merits of sales force incentives against, say, an increase in advertising costs. It would be pointless to spend on advertising if an incentive could do the job for less without alerting the competition to what was going on. Experience could show that it pays off to include incentives in the marketing plan.

The sales promotion activity plan

The sales promotion activity plan will include a planned programme of promotional events, customer sales seminars, exhibitions, customer incentives and salesmen incentives.

When thinking of sales force incentives it makes sense to synchronise the incentive with another sales activity such as a customer incentive campaign or sales promotion event. For example, a promotional event aimed at interesting new potential customers can be linked with a sales force incentive which encourages salesmen to follow up all the names in the attendance register with perhaps greater diligence than usual. It is an unfortunate fact (proved time after time by research surveys) that many of the customers who attend sales seminars or visit exhibitions are not subsequently followed up efficiently by members of the company's sales team. An incentive helps to maximise the sales opportunities created in this way, and result in a much more cost effective promotion/exhibition.

One example of how a salesman incentive was successfully linked with a customer promotion is the experience of an electronic component manufacturer. The company regularly exhibited their products at trade shows, and over the years enjoyed a steady return in terms of new business from new customers. In addition, many of their existing customers whose buyers and engineers visited the trade shows also placed additional orders, sometimes for lines which had not previously been purchased from that manufacturer. Then a new company sales manager decided to exploit to the full the opportunities which he believed may have been missed by previous follow up exercises. He introduced a sales incentive scheme designed to motivate his salesmen to increase their efforts to win business from potential new customers who had indicated an interest in the company's products during the trade show. In practice, what happened was that the salesmen now paid much more attention to every visitor to their stand, regardless of the status of the individual and regardless of whether they already had a good contact with the customer. Result – customers who had previously only bought one product were urged to buy other products in the range. Casual visitors to the stand, having no direct influence on the buying decision, were pumped for every tiny piece of information which might assist in preparing a new approach which could lead to the introduction of another product.

Also, potential new customers who had previously been classified as 'messers' (i.e. visiting the show to enjoy a day out) were more thoroughly investigated before this judgement was exercised.

Furthermore, salesmen on stand duty showed a much greater keenness and enthusiasm in approaching visitors to their exhibition stand. (How often do we see a couldn't care less attitude by salesmen at these trade shows?) A 15 per cent increase in resultant business was achieved by this manufacturer who now regularly introduces sales incentive schemes to tie in with promotional events.

Monitoring and measuring

How can we be sure that an increase in sales can be attributed to an incentive campaign? The short answer to the question is that we can't. However, experience is a great tester and if sales regularly go up during or immediately following a sales incentive, it's fair to assume that it has been effective. Of course sales can be monitored and measured, but as previously mentioned, sales could have been affected by some other external factor such as an upsurge in market demand, or production problems at a competitor's factory.

If we believe that the main influence over sales results is the attitude and enthusiasm of a salesman, then this is something that can be monitored and measured. For example, during a sales incentive contest one would expect salesmen to be extra keen to respond to customer enquiries. Methods of testing salesmen's attitude and enthusiasm can be easily arranged. A 'mystery shopper' exercise using standard tests and key questions can record results (say a points score) before and after an incentive is introduced.

Telephone shopping is another simple way of monitoring salesmen's performance. One car distributor often uses this as a means of checking the effectiveness of sales incentive schemes. On one particular occasion the salesmen were encouraged to compete by putting pre-set questions to every potential customer who telephoned the showroom to enquire about a new car. They had an enquiry note pad which contained six questions which the salesmen were required to ask each customer. The winning salesman won a prize for his success in obtaining most information from most customers, starting with the customer's name and address. One determined salesman asked a reticent mystery caller for his name and address five times during the course of a telephone enquiry. Prior to introducing the incentive many of the salesmen were not bothering to get names and addresses of potential customers. Certainly it was exceptional for any salesman to ask twice for a customer's name and address. Asking five times still didn't guarantee extra business, but it did demonstrate the new enthusiasm of the sales team.

Monitoring sales work rate can provide another method of measuring the effectiveness of a sales incentive. Many sales managers use sales force control systems which report regularly on the call rate and prospecting activities of their salesmen. This measure of 'sales productivity' or effective call rate, is based on the percentage of real selling time a salesman spends face to face with prospective customers. In theory, increasing the amount of real selling time will result in a greater number of orders. Introducing an incentive to stimulate call rate should be easily measurable by making a comparison of records before, during and after the period of the incentive campaign. Previous ratios showing percentage of order rate to call rate can also be measured to check that the incentive is motivating salesmen towards making more effective sales calls and not simply playing a numbers game.

Refining and improving sales incentive schemes

As a general rule, having found a winning formula, it's best to stick to it. It's probably easier to look at the failures and analyse why they went wrong than it is to improve on a previous success. Probably the least efficient element in a sales incentive campaign is communication. Many failed incentives failed because they were not promoted vigorously enough to those people who were expected to respond to the incentive. Even the most attractive incentive scheme can be enhanced by being imaginatively sold to the sales people.

For example an incentive offering a prize holiday can be made more attractive by obtaining holiday brochures, maps of the resort area, information about interesting events in the area, post cards sent from the resort. One enterprising sales manager included invitations to a party in Hong Kong to members of his team competing for a holiday there. Another element in a sales incentive contest that should constantly be improved is the communication of news relating to the incentive. Salesmen should be informed fast about results and progress. It's no motivation at all when a salesman is fed with information weeks after the event.

Running sales incentives

When to press the 'Go' button

The very essence of a successful incentive is selecting the right time. In so many fields, timing is of crucial importance. The professional soldier, the professional actor, the professional footballer and the professional salesman all rely on their ability to apply perfect timing. Likewise, the manager must be professional in choosing the right time to switch on an imaginative incentive. This can make all the difference between real success and mediocrity. To ensure that an incentive does its job the following questions must be answered satisfactorily:

Is it the right time to motivate the salesmen by an incentive? Are the customers likely to respond to an intensive sales campaign? Can the product be made available in sufficient quantity to meet a possible upsurge in sales? Do market conditions indicate a potential requirement for the product? Can the company's administrative staff efficiently handle the paperwork necessary to maintain close communications and statistics necessary for monitoring the results of the incentive campaign?

Consider the customer first. He may already be swamped by special offers, discount deals, coupon redemptions, six for the price of five deals, trial offers, and new product launches. You and your competitors between you may have tried a whole range of ideas to push your products to the fore. It might be a refreshing change for the customer if he is approached by a professional salesman with an enthusiastic positive attitude. He may be more inclined to be influenced by enthusiastic sales effort than gimmicky giveaways. The competition, continuing to peddle the same old discount deals and special offers, could be taken by surprise, as they will be unaware that the company has done anything different. The sales manager must use his judgement and knowledge of the market and competition to decide exactly when to introduce his sales campaign.

Timing is also important for the salesman. For example, an incentive introduced during a holiday season, or when territories have just been re-arranged, or when product delivery schedules are erratic, could have much less impact. People buy people before they buy products, and the effect of an alert, highly motivated salesforce can give the company a selling edge to beat competitors.

A sales incentive focused on promoting sales of a selected product is frequently timed to coincide either with a new product launch or with an old product run out. It's important to ensure that adequate supplies will be available during the incentive period. It may also be useful to consider timing a customer promotion to link up with a sales incentive campaign. For example, a manufacturer could advertise a 'golden opportunity' to his customers and at the same time launch a 'golden opportunity' incentive for his salesmen.

Market conditions can also influence decisions on the timing of incentives. It may be inappropriate to run an incentive campaign during seasonal peaks in market demand, particularly if the company resources are stretched to cope with distribution or finance. It may be better instead, to consider a sales incentive out of season when customers need more persuasion to buy.

Administration also has to be capable of handling the extra paperwork that may be generated by a sales incentive campaign. It could be bad timing to run an incentive during a busy end of year accounting period, or stocktaking, or budgeting exercise. These are important factors to take into account when planning incentive activities.

Leadership and motivation

Leadership is a very important management quality. The most sophisticated marketing plans, the most creative incentive schemes, the finest communication systems, the cleverest monitoring devices, won't work effectively unless managers accept their responsibilities as leaders.

Salesmen need firm leadership if they are to achieve the highest levels of performance. A verbal pat on the back or short note of encouragement to the salesman in the field can work wonders for morale and motivation. Salesmen particularly respond to leadership by example. Good leaders are invariably good motivators.

One experienced sales manager, responsible for a sales force employed by a large national company, developed a habit of writing frequent short notes to his salesmen, always looking for ways in which he could congratulate or compliment them. The response he received nearly always repaid his efforts. He began this practice and continued to take the time and trouble to write to his men in this way over a period of many years. Early on, he realised how much it meant to one salesman when the man's wife mentioned that her husband often brought the notes home and proudly showed them to her. It made her proud too and enhanced her feelings about the manager and the company. Periodically, the company ran sales incentive

schemes, which were invariably successful because of the
enthusiastic support they received from the salesmen's
families. Praising sales achievements as well as rewarding them can be an excellent no cost motivator. The manager who takes the time to think about encouraging
his salesmen is applying one of the finest motivational
techniques.

Public relations and incentives

Part of the pleasure of winning is letting everyone know
about it. Sales success can sometimes be publicised in
media such as house magazines and trade journals. Where
this is possible it's well worth the effort and the relatively
low cost. Customers like to be identified with successful
companies and successful people. A big order or a new contract could possibly affect the future of members of a company workforce. This is great news for the local press and
trade press and can have spin off benefits in other areas
such as recruitment – salesmen are more likely to be at-
tracted to a company which they perceive to be successful.

Reviewing incentives that failed

Talking to salesmen about previous incentive campaigns
can be an enlightening exercise. One company commis-
sioned a survey of salesmen's opinions by employing a
research organisation to interview a cross-section of
salesmen, taken from a variety of national companies.
They approached only those companies who had operated
sales incentive schemes which had either failed al-
together or enjoyed only moderate success. The following
questions were included in the survey. The answers repre-
sent the typical comments which were made by the majority of the salesmen involved:

Question: 'Do you like the use of incentives in your company and are you pleased to have the opportunity of winning prizes?'

Answer: 'Yes, incentives do add that extra bit of interest to the job. Frankly, I don't take them too seriously. Winning is more a matter of luck than anything else.'

Q: 'What incentive prizes do you like best?'

A: 'I prefer exotic holidays, but often the problem is that we can't take the family. My wife prefers merchandise awards, but we often end up using these to get ordinary household items which take away the excitement for me.'

Q: 'If you had to choose between (1) cash, (2) holidays, (3) merchandise, (4) bonds or (5) a really first class educational/training course as a prize, which would you choose?'

A: 'I've never been offered the option of (5), but it sounds interesting. I think my selection would be first (2) second (5) third (3) and I'd bracket (1) and (4) together.

Q: 'What is the main purpose of the incentive schemes introduced by your company?'

A: 'All they ever think about is increasing sales and profit.'

Q: 'Have you ever manipulated your sales results to help you win a contest?'

A: 'Of course, it's part of the game for us salesmen. Sometimes we get together at the start and decide to pool our winnings and have an equal share out afterwards.'

Q: 'Do you honestly think that sales incentives work?'

A: 'No, in the main they don't. In fairness, I suppose there have been occasions when I've worked extra hard because of an incentive. Particularly if I've been near to winning a top prize.'

Q: 'What do you think of cash as an incentive prize?'

A: 'The first time I won a cash prize I really thought cash was best. Then at the end of the month they stopped the tax and I was thoroughly disgruntled. Now I prefer benefits in kind and if the tax man catches up with me, at least the tax is spread evenly over the year.'

Q: 'Have the incentive contests which your company introduced usually been fair to all the salesmen?'

A: 'No, there always seems to be an argument over allocation of targets. That's why we often get together to pool the winnings. Incentives based on individual performance are most popular with us, but the company has tried a combination of individual and team competitions which seemed to go quite well.'

Q: 'Do you ever let customers know when a sales incentive campaign is running?'

A: 'Yes, depending on my relationship with the customer. Sometimes they help me by giving me extra orders, or bringing orders forward.'

Q: 'Generally, are you kept well informed about the progress of sales competitions during the period of the competition?'

A: 'No, often hardly at all. I sometimes get the impression that results are hastily cobbled together just to get rid of the nuisance of administration. Mind you, I have seen this used to advantage by some salesmen who take advantage of the situation by duplicating orders or issuing credit notes a month after the event.'

Q: 'From your own knowledge, and contacts with other salesmen, which industries seem to make the most regular use of incentives?'

A: 'I believe incentives are widely used in the insurance business. Also the motor trade seem to offer a lot of incentives to salesmen. My impression is that they offer incentives in conjunction with other promotions which seems a good idea. Computer salesmen also seem to be offered exotic incentives, which surprises me in view of their very high earnings.'

Q: 'Are incentives operated in your company as a part of a planned programme, or are they introduced in *ad hoc* fashion?'

A: 'They're usually rushed in as a panic measure to try to cure a short term problem. Sometimes, management set the targets too high and then have to reduce them to more realistic levels.'

Q: 'If you were a sales manager would you use incentives to motivate your sales force?'

A: 'Yes, but I'd try to design sales contests which were fair to everybody and I'd make damn sure they weren't fiddling sales figures to win prizes.'

The results of this survey of salesmen's opinions could dismay the sales manager who happens to be contemplating using incentives for the first time. However, what these results really indicate are that managers generally do a poor job of running sales incentives. There's no reason why properly planned and efficiently organised incentives can't be effective as a motivational tool. Much depends on creating the right conditions for an incentive to work. Then a good manager can get on with the job of making it work.

One sales incentive horror story is worth repeating. It came to light during discussion with a group of salesmen about incentives operated by their companies. This was an incentive introduced by a motor manufacturer aimed at increasing sales of a particular make of car. By offering a special incentive to vehicle contract hire and leasing salesmen, it was hoped to influence them into guiding buyers' decisions, thus improving penetration in this growth sector of the market. Great. The first mistake was that the glossy catalogue of merchandise, details of the incentive, and claim forms were issued to the lucky salesmen at the end of March. However, the incentive had started on 1 January and the salesmen were entitled to claim prize points (for merchandise) for the three months January–March. The extravagant campaign was to run for a whole year, and the opportunities for amassing a hoard of points were exciting indeed. Then silence. No further communication. No news bulletin. No announcement. No publicity. Nothing – until August. Then a duplicated letter went out to all participants from the manufac-

turer's sales director, urging them to sell more Brand X
and earn themselves some jolly good prizes. The forms to
claim prize points for use in ordering merchandise were
'following shortly'. (They arrived about a month later.) A
final letter was sent out in December announcing the end
of the incentive campaign, and advising salesmen to sub-
mit claims. It took another two months to vet and approve
all claims. The prizes were finally ordered and delivered
in April, but not before a number of irate and disappointed
salesmen had become thoroughly disenchanted with the
car manufacturer.

Probably that was an exception, they had a lot of problems that year! The prizes were certainly attractive.
Maybe somebody decided they were too attractive to promote during the incentive period. Then after the campaign nothing more was heard. No publicity pictures
of smiling salesmen receiving their hard won awards,
nothing – which about sums up the effectiveness of the
campaign.

Reports of sales targets being increased after the start
of an incentive scheme are also indicative of the disas-
trously slapdash way in which some managers approach
the subject. The lessons should be very clear.

Conclusion

The changing status of the salesman

Today, business managers have to consider very carefully the economics of employing salesmen. Standards have been improving rapidly and salesmen are expected to be professional. Many companies insist on qualifications such as a university degree in marketing or business studies. Salesmen are enjoying a better status in their companies. They are expected to accept a much greater responsibility for generating profit and keeping people in employment. As a result, the selling profession is attracting more intelligent people.

The modern salesman is now more likely to receive a comprehensive remuneration package which includes benefits such as a company car, expenses, private medical care, pension, and a high basic salary plus commission or bonus. Many companies take the view that this calibre of employee should maintain a high level of self motivation without any added incentives. In reality, this doesn't happen. In fact, it's doubtful if many salesmen work to anywhere near the maximum of their time and ability. They probably work more efficiently and perform more effectively, but they could, nevertheless, work harder.

Motivation – a management art

To motivate today's ~~salesmen~~ team probably requires more sophisticated management techniques than ever before. However, the rewards for success still make the goal well worth striving for. Motivation is still a very important part of managing. It is important because when used properly, it's a cost effective tool which can make extra profit for the company. It's vital to keep a ~~sales force~~ team motivated and working hard at all times.

Buying incentive expertise

Selecting incentives can be a time consuming and often difficult process. There are many professional incentive consultants who can be called in to give advice and assistance in designing and operating incentive schemes. The growth of incentive marketing companies has proved the value of this service during the past twenty years or so in the UK. The ideal type of agency is not biased towards any particular type of product or leisure service, and therefore, is more likely to produce an incentive package to match the needs of the client company and its sales team. However, many company managers still prefer to design and run their own incentive schemes which probably accounts for a low success rate and an all too common prejudice against incentives. As the calibre of the people coming into the selling profession improves, the pressures are likely to force sales managers to be more professional themselves in the techniques of applying incentives as a motivational tool.

The last word

The following comment comes from a sales manager employed by a large motor parts and accessory manufacturer. He is responsible for 72 salesmen working through a national distribution network.

'During my years doing this job, I've been involved in many campaigns aimed at stimulating extra sales. I've had a good record of success. My own conclusion is that there are basic rules which should be applied to every campaign. The purpose, as far as we're concerned, should be to control the selling efforts into selling the products we want sold, and to introduce an element of fun into the job. We always use incentives in conjunction with customer based promotion programmes. Before I'd use sales incentives, I'd want to be sure that I had a well controlled sales force, with a thorough knowledge of the product. I'd take care to give them specific targets, and I'd want an efficient monitoring system to check on their performance. They must also be properly equipped with the selling tools to enable them to give a first class presentation of our product to every customer. I give considerable thought to beating competition in our business. I'd like to annihilate them by motivating my salesmen to work like dervishes twenty-four hours a day! When I use sales incentives that's the kind of success I dream about.'

Directory of incentive marketing and sales promotion organisations

The following list of consultants and suppliers is intended to provide the reader with a useful contact list of companies who can be of service. It's by no means a comprehensive list, as there are literally hundreds of companies in the business. An annual Buyers' Guide, published by *Incentive Marketing and Sales Promotion* magazine contains about 200 pages of suppliers' lists and advertisements (address below).

Publishers

Incentive Marketing and Sales Promotion
Maclaren Publishers Ltd., P.O. Box 109, Davis House, 69/77 High Street, Croydon CR9 1QH. Tel. 01–688 7788

Professional Associations

British Premium Merchandise Association
21–25 Lower Stone Street, Maidstone, Kent ME15 6YT.
Tel. 0622 671081–2

Institute of Sales Promotion
548 Chiswick High Road, London W4 5RG. Tel. 01–995
4686

Consultants and agents

These companies create or advise on the creation of trade
and consumer promotions and incentives for client companies.

The EF MacDonald Co. Ltd.
56 Davies Street, London W1Y 1LB. Tel. 01–499 8192

Motivation and Marketing
30 Eastbourne Terrace, London W2 6LD. Tel. 01–402
7617

Performance Awards (1980) Ltd.
1 High Street, Edgware, Middx. HA8 7DE. Tel. 01–952
7740

The Sales Machine Ltd.
22 James Street, Covent Garden, London WC2E 8NS. Tel.
01–240 3027

Incentive and conference travel

BITA (Business Incentive & Awards) Ltd.
17 Clifford Street, London W1X 1RB. Tel. 01–439 3661

A wide range varying from UK venues and European
weekend breaks to around the world tours.

Debenhams
1 Welbeck Street, London W1 1DR. Tel. 01–499 6604
Debenhams/Exchange Holiday Tokens. £25 units.

Ellerman Incentive
Travel House, 14 High Street, Pinner, Middx. HA5 5PP.
Tel. 01–868 3725

Embassy Hotels (Grandstand Promotional Service)
Station Street, Burton on Trent, Staffs. Tel. 0283 6658
Incentive travel arrangements for sporting events in the
UK.

The EF MacDonald Travel Co.
58 Davies Street, London W1Y 1LB. Tel. 01-499 8192

Maritz Travel
315 Oxford Street, London W1R 2BQ. Tel. 01–499 3922

Page & Moy Ltd.
136 London Road, Leicester LE2 1EN. Tel. 0533 542000

Performance Awards (1980) Ltd.
1 High Street, Edgware, Middx. HA8 7DE. Tel. 01–952
7740

P & O Travel
Conference and Incentive Division, 87 Jermyn Street,
London SW1. Tel. 01-930 9883

Vouchers for promotional use

These companies issue vouchers, bonds and other award
currencies as premiums and incentives for promotional
and motivational activities.

Argos Distributors Ltd.
112 Station Road, Edgware, Middx. Tel. 01–951 1363

The Boots Co. Ltd.
Incentive and Awards Division, Gift Vouchers Department, City Gate, Nottingham NG2 3AA. Tel. 0602 48522
ext. 6355

Embassy Hotels (Hushaway Breaks)
Station Street, Burton on Trent, Staffs. Tel. 0283 66587

J.H. Dewhurst Ltd.
Dewhurst House, 24–30 West Smithfield, London EC1A
9DL. Tel. 01–236 1981

Peter Dominic Ltd.
Vintner House, River Way, Harlow, Essex. Tel. 0279
26801

Ellerman Travel Bonds
Travel House, 14 High Street, Pinner, Middx. HA5 5PP.
Tel. 01-868 3725

Habitat Designs Ltd.
Hithcroft Road, Wallingford, Oxon. Tel. 0491 35000

Halford Ltd.
Ickneild Street Drive, Washford West, Redditch, Worcs.
B98 0DE. Tel. 0527 27601

Hornes (Menswear)
Durigo House, King Edward's Road, London E9 7SG. Tel.
01–986 3166

H. Samuel Ltd.
Hunter Road, Birmingham B19 1DS. Tel. 021–554 3871

Supreme Awards
88–92 Earls Court Road, Kensington, London W8 6EH.
Tel. 01–938 1041
Multi-usage vouchers, travel, fashion, music, sport,
leisure, wining, dining, hotel accommodation.

Victoria Wine
Brook House, Chertsey Road, Woking, Surrey. Tel. 04862
5066

F.W. Woolworth & Co. Ltd.
Shopping Vouchers Division, 1264–66, London Road,
Norbury, London SW16 4EF. Tel. 01–764 5050

Workforce motivation

The companies listed below provide workforce motivation programmes for clients' employees.

BITA (Business Incentives & Travel Awards) Ltd.
17 Clifford Street, London W1X 1RB. Tel. 01–439 3661
Use a combination of own voucher system BITA Bonds and holidays and incentive travel.

Motivation and Marketing
30 Eastbourne Terrace, London W2 6LD. Tel. 01–402 7617
Thirty different retail store vouchers from stock. Holiday vouchers from stock. Extensive range of merchandise and premiums.

Sales Promotion and Merchandising Ltd.
Penthouse Suite, Turriff Building, Great West Road, Brentford, Middx. TW8 9HZ. Tel. 01–560 2257